All Over
the Map

All Over the Map

Rethinking American Regions

Edward L. Ayers
Patricia Nelson Limerick
Stephen Nissenbaum
Peter S. Onuf

The Johns Hopkins University Press
Baltimore and London

© 1996 The Johns Hopkins University Press
All rights reserved. Published 1996
Printed in the United States of America on acid-free paper
05 04 03 02 01 00 99 98   5 4 3 2

The Johns Hopkins University Press
2715 North Charles Street
Baltimore, Maryland 21218-4319

Library of Congress Cataloging-in-Publication Data will be found at
the end of this book.
A catalog record for this book is available from the British Library.

ISBN 0-8018-5206-4
ISBN 0-8018-5392-3 pbk.

Contents

Preface

American identities are rooted in places on the national map, regions that are related to one another by directional signifiers: North/South, East/West. In these regions, time converges with space; the bright promise of a bountiful future comes down to Earth. Generic Americans become real people in particular places: they put down roots, acquire accents, assume historic burdens. Even as we keep moving, all over the map, we cherish memories of the regions we come from.

But where do *regions* come from, and what makes them seem so real? It is important to remember that the national compass that gives us our bearings, the map that defines where we stand, is itself an imaginative construction, an icon of nationhood. Without the nation there could be no regions; without the whole there could be no parts. And what makes any region seem distinctive is differences that only make sense in a common context, in competition for relative advantage and influence.

However much regions define one another, the definitions are always slippery. Throughout their history, Americans have argued over where one region ends and another begins. Westward expansion sustained confusion throughout the nineteenth century, as the "West" itself moved west (from trans-Appalachia across the Mississippi) and Northerners and Southerners struggled to project their versions of American civilization and regional identity across the continent. Americans were mapmakers, imposing boundaries and property lines on a supposedly virgin landscape. Where those boundaries ran and who created and controlled the institutions within them made all the difference in the world. In the antebellum years, when regional antagonisms ran deepest, the limits of those regions were most controversial. It was precisely because Northerners and Southerners could *not* define a mutual boundary and could not agree on how to apportion their common property that they finally resorted to arms. Unable to distinguish regional from national identity, Americans found themselves—and one another—all over the map.

Our political geography is considerably tidier these days. This does not mean that, having learned better, we now eschew regional identities. The opposite is more nearly true. The Civil War has given a kind of *gravitas*, a tragic historic weight, to regional differences that early generations of Americans wore more lightly, and exploited more opportunistically. It simultaneously functions as the great, monitory lesson in the forging of a national identity—never, never again will Americans slaughter one another—and, particularly for Southerners, as the glorious apotheosis of regional identity, all the more glorious for the war's apparent futility. Through such logic, regionalism was rejoined to nationalism. Not only the South rose again under its aegis but so too did the West, the great regional casualty in the struggle over the extension of slavery into the territories. This volume explores the multiple meanings that Americans have invested in their regional identities. These identities are so centrally important because they could never be—and can never be—taken for granted.

This book had its origins as the Harrison Lectures at the Johns Hopkins University in the spring of 1993. Ayers, Limerick, and Onuf received the warm hospitality of the Department of History for three days, enjoying gracious entertainment and friendly but rigorous questioning. We would especially like to thank Louis Galambos for the invitation and Richard Goldthwaite, then chair of the department, for organizing things so smoothly.

E.A. and P.O.

All Over
the Map

Introduction

*Edward L. Ayers
and Peter S. Onuf*

Where do American ideas about regions and regional identity
come from? This is a question we rarely ask ourselves, because
the answer seems so obvious. Regions with distinctive climates,
geographies, cultures, and histories are simply "there"; they provide the framework for understanding who we are, what has happened to us, and what we can look forward to. Patriotic rhetoric
and song invoke distinctive landscapes "from sea to shining sea,"
embracing and transcending regional diversity. Maps of the United
States, cartographic icons of nationhood, draw our attention outward, across the continent, away from the centers of population
and power and toward the different places we all come from.
Thinking ourselves across space, we think ourselves backward in
time, imaginatively returning to particular places in an idealized
past. American geography thus recapitulates American history;
history is immanent in the distinctive character and culture of the
nation's diverse regions. This dialectic of space and time, mobility
and nostalgia, has shaped our understanding of the role of regions
in American history.

Historians and cultural geographers have a vested interest in exaggerating popular ignorance, and their own importance. In their
efforts to reconstruct the past or to illuminate the past's continuing
presence in our culture, these scholars take their stand against the
homogenizing, ultimately obliterating impact of modernity on his-

torical memory. But modern Americans do not lack a sense of history, historic places, or distinctive regions. What we lack is a sense of how regional identity shaped, and has been shaped by, national identity—of how we have spatialized time and historicized space. This book explores the evolution of ideas about region in the United States from the country's founding to the present day. The individual chapters are essays, not comprehensive surveys of regional characteristics. The first chapter explores the political framework that virtually guaranteed that regions would come to play a key role in the political history of the federal republic, that regions would be pitted against one another in ways that would jeopardize the survival of the union. The other three essays are written with two sets of questions in mind: the concerns of particular parts of the country and the broader problems of understanding regions in general. Students of the American South tend to focus on topics different from those of interest to students of New England or the American West, but we believe that everyone can benefit from thinking about the language and assumptions we use to think about region in the first place.

There long has been in the United States a cyclical process of forgetfulness and rediscovery of the idea of region. In the twentieth century, for example, "regionalism" was vibrant in the 1930s but passé in the 1950s and 1960s. Since the 1970s there has been a spate of new studies of region, in many disciplines, regarding many different places. The resurgence of interest in and loyalty to region is reflected in the impassioned localism of environmentalism and historic preservation; the new regionalism appears, too, in the form of regional magazines and festivals, in the packaging of local particularities by tourist boards and chambers of commerce. In academic circles, the new regionalism has been manifested in a fascination with local history and in the proliferation of state humanities councils and regional studies centers. Regionalism grows, too, by default, as many seem to have lost faith in national innocence and the national state, have grown dubious of a transcendent national character and American exceptionalism. In an age of disillusionment with big structures and transhistorical dreams, many Americans have apparently decided that places closer to home deserve more of their loyalty.[1]

Despite the renaissance of regionalism and the ever-growing sophistication with which we can study and measure regional characteristics, many discussions of region, popular and academic, seem to revolve around an extraordinarily persistent set of assumptions. One assumption is that regional identity is at heart an inheritance from the past, a moral and intellectual "heritage" that, if it is to endure, must be preserved from the ravages of modern life. To many people, it appears that there was a time in the past when each region was most fully itself: the Old South, the Old West, pristine New England. Since then, we are told, there has been a relentless adulteration and watering down of these places by the forces of modern life.

Another assumption is that the North, South, and West naturally developed out of variations in the American landscape. Regional differences in people appear to be reflections of regional differences in land and climate. Americans tend to think in nature metaphors—cold, rocky New England creating cold, rocky New Englanders; hot and humid Dixie creating hot-tempered men and dewy women; the big skies and wide-open spaces of the West creating independent men and self-sufficient women. When people warn of the demise of regions they usually couch their warning in images of landscapes lost, of battlefields desecrated, of paradise paved. To lose distinctive features of the land is to lose the depth and salience of region, or so most of us assume.

Yet if Americans speak of region only to speak of loss, regions do not seem to be disappearing. Accents are not being scrubbed away by mass media. Historical memory has never been so lovingly cherished and burnished. Stereotypes, negative and positive, have not diminished. People carry in their heads quite powerful and uniform mental maps of the United States. Americans refuse to let regional identity die, because it offers something that appears to be hard to find in a mass society: a form of identity that promises to transcend ethnic boundaries, to unite people across generations. Yet the worry persists that mere desire might not be enough to keep regions alive, that our very level of self-consciousness is an indication of the death of real, natural regions.

This book is an exploration of these notions. We critically examine the language with which Americans talk about regions not because we want to destroy attachment to those places but because we want to be more honest with ourselves about the meanings we invest in them. Regions may be in danger not only from malls and cable television but also from attempts to freeze places in time or to define some particular component of a region as its essence, leading regionalists to despair when that essence seems to be disappearing. It is better, we think, to recognize that regions have *always* been complex and unstable constructions, generated by constantly evolving systems of government, economy, migration, event, and culture. Once we see that regions were never bounded and complete entities, we can see how it is that regions may survive far longer than people imagine.

We are skeptical of those who want to lay claim to some kind of ownership of regional identity, to identify *their* "heritage" as the genuine one. We think it is important to see regions more expansively, to include more people as genuine participants in the creation of regional life. While regional identity can and often does involve an explicit or implicit critique of people elsewhere within the nation, especially those who live in the metropole, regional identity is usually more about belonging than it is about exclusion. People seem able to "become" Southerners or Westerners in a way they cannot become black or white, Italian or Puerto Rican. Cowboy hats and blue jeans are worn by both Mexican-Americans and Anglos; hunting and fishing appeal to both black and white Southerners; professional sports enable white-collar and working-class people across New England to identify with one another and with their region.

It may be useful to measure regional identity according to a set of distinctive attributes or attitudes—in vocabulary, say, or food preferences, or ideas about abortion or guns. Such studies in sociology and cultural geography have gone a long way toward showing the continuing vitality of regional differences. But they sometimes imply that history is a nonrenewable resource, a reservoir steadily drained of its content. Regional differences often appear as artifacts, holdovers, cultural lags waiting for the homogenizing effects of mass media and transportation to erase them. The authors of this book resist such assumptions; to us, it seems that history holds many more meanings than can be accounted for by any measurable characteristics of current residents of the region. History creates all sorts of latent meanings in a place, meanings that may not be visible at any given moment but that can quickly come to the surface as events change. Rather than a reservoir, stagnant and bounded, history is more like a complex system of underground rivers and springs, creating its own subterranean pressures.[2]

Similarly, we would encourage readers to rethink the role of business, commerce, and industry in regional histories. Since at least the Civil War the market seems to have been the most corrosive and homogenizing force in America. People tend to think that the only places where difference survives are the places where the market has not performed its full work—on isolated islands, in mountain valleys, or on distant farmsteads. But just as markets played a key role in creating regions in the first place, production and exchange giving land and climate their first regional meanings, so they continue to make regions salient today. The economic limitations and possibilities of one era can be and often are quickly reversed in the next, a useless mountain becoming a mine, a useless mining town later becoming a ski resort. Some archaic institutions of the market have become widespread symbols of American regions. The old fishing village, the sign-covered general store, and the windblown gas station are among the most common symbols of New England, the South, and the West, respectively, testimony to the power of the market in earlier versions of those regions. Coal mines, ghost towns, and bed-and-breakfast inns have not always been around, but they have become icons of particular American places. Stock-car tracks, gambling casinos, and Italian pizzerias, all market-driven products of the twentieth century, are becoming regional artifacts today even though they seem to violate the "traditional" canons of esthetics and authenticity so cherished by regionalists.

The authors of this book do not see regions as areas filled with a certain kind of cultural ether, but rather as places where discrete, though related, structures intersect and interact in particular patterns. The region *is* climate and land; it *is* a particular set of relations between various ethnic groups; it *is* a relation to the federal government and economy; it *is* a set of shared cultural styles. But each of these elements, even the influence of land and climate, is constantly changing. Accordingly, their relationships with one another also are constantly changing. The result of these changing relationships is regional history. Present-day Southerners, Westerners, and New Englanders, we believe, can best connect with their pasts not so much through some unbroken and unsullied heritage but rather by, as it were, comparing notes, experiences, with those who came before, with those who lived on the same land when it was something different.

Historians of every period of American history have concerned themselves with region, though in widely varying ways. For historians of the twentieth century, region is often a matter of government policy, of voting patterns, of shifting economic fortunes. For historians of the nineteenth century, questions about region tend to be questions about national identity, about the relationships between slavery, frontiers, and industry. For historians of the eighteenth century, the Revolution and nation-building tend to be preoccupying problems. For historians of the seventeenth century, questions of origins, of the migration and evolution of culture, are the major concern. While the essays in this book cut across all these eras, it might be useful to take our bearings in the earliest periods first.

Divergent approaches to early American history, one focusing on colonial beginnings, the other offering fresh perspectives on nation-building and national identity, have brought the problem of region to the historiographical fore. Colonial historians have given the new nation multiple pasts, grounded in the cultures and experiences of diverse settlement areas; meanwhile, Revolutionary historians have sought to show how colonists with such a wide array of local interests and loyalties could come to discover a common, national identity as "Americans." Thanks to these scholars, we have a much better understanding of the genealogy of regions and regional identities as well as of the Revolutionary origins of nationhood and national identity. But we have yet to bring these literatures together in a completely satisfying fashion, notwithstanding a recent flurry of ambitious and impressive efforts at synthesis.[3] Looking forward, the Revolutionary generation confronted the problem of integrating localities and regions in effective union;

modern scholars look backward and seek to balance the claims of the little communities that constituted colonial America and of the new national community the Americans invented. Colonial historians emphasize the social and cultural adaptations of European settlers to New World conditions. Working in a transatlantic, early modern European historiographical framework, they have shifted attention away from independence and nationmaking and toward the founding of colonial societies. By providing authoritative expositions of the spread of settlement and culture patterns from diverse regional "hearths," these writers have both Europeanized and regionalized the story of American beginnings.[4] In their work, "Europe" itself has dissolved into a patchwork of local regions, still only loosely organized around and subject to emerging central governments or metropolitan economies. The colonialists' emphasis on distinctive colonial origins and adaptations legitimates and reinvigorates the classic dichotomies—setting Massachusetts Bay against Virginia, New England against the Chesapeake, North against South—that have structured popular as well as scholarly understanding of national history. The irresistible conclusion is that regional identities antedate the new nation's founding and therefore were as much a given for the founders as they are for us today.

Revolutionary historians, focusing on political ideology and popular mobilization, give us a radically different account of the new nation's beginnings.[5] Seeking to explain how so many Americans could bring themselves to declare their independence, these historians invoked a much more malleable and manipulable notion of "culture" (as discourse or ideology) than have their colonialist colleagues, who were more impressed with deep structures and durable patterns. The ideological historians have devoted much of their energy to criticizing one another for exaggerating the classical republican or liberal sources and character of Revolutionary political thought. While this great historiographical controversy has complicated, confused, and conflated the original positions of its protagonists, its net effect has been to widen the gap between colonial and national history. Thus, where colonial historiography gave an authoritative pedigree to regional difference and the persistence of local identities, Revolutionary historians underscored the novelty of American republicanism (whatever its ideological sources) and the inventiveness of the founders in conceiving and constructing a new national politics.

In the traditional narrative of American history, independence was the logical outcome of colonial history, the culmination of an extended apprenticeship in self-government. In the wake of the new historiography of colonial and Revolutionary America, the story no longer seems so straightforward. Where did American nationhood come from, if its seeds were not planted with the first settlements? And what does the history of nation-making have to do with the lives of particular people whose interests and identities were so closely tied to the histories of distinctive local communities?

The Revolution had a profound impact on local and regional identities in the British American colonies. A new nationality was not simply superimposed on older, enduring communal loyalties. To the contrary, independence brought questions of loyalty and allegiance to new levels of consciousness and contentiousness, encouraging Americans to redefine their rights and interests as citizens of local communities, states, and the union as a whole. Traditional ways of acting and thinking could provide only limited guidance as Revolutionaries constructed new collective identities and projected them into new and unfamiliar contexts. Interstate conflict precipitated new concepts of statehood. In similar fashion, the development of regional consciousness was predicated on awareness of *other* regions in a competitive political context.

We do not question the persistence of regionally specific social and cultural patterns across the Revolutionary period and throughout American history. But the key issue for students of regionalism is to explain why some cultural distinctions come to matter, while so many do not, in the construction of collective identities. Persistent folkways might continue to define the texture of daily life for most Americans, but a consciousness of difference would give them new value and significance. Regional idiosyncrasies would only become conspicuous within a national framework as they rose to the level of self-conscious reflection and manipulation.

Regions defined one another in a nation of regions. This process of reciprocal definition did not inexorably lead to conflict, disunion, and war. Advocates of regional interests in the new federal republic did not conceive of themselves as secret separatists or conditional unionists. From the Revolutionaries' perspective, local loyalties constituted the threshold of an enlightened patriotism that ultimately embraced all freedom-loving Americans across the continent. American nationalism was not predicated on suppressing and supplanting these multiple, overlapping loyalties, but rather on creating a complex constitutional regime that would secure the equal rights of localities as well as of individuals. Localists and sectionalists could thus portray themselves as patriotic Americans, while impugning the patriotism of politicians from *other* sections who threatened their vital interests and therefore the integrity of the union itself.

Scholars may define the boundaries of regional cultures with some degree of precision. In doing so, they have the advantage over their subjects, whose sense of where they were situated—with respect to other "peoples" in other "regions"—was subject to constant redefinition. The great sectional crisis leading to the Civil War has made "North" and "South" seem like timeless entities, distinctive regions that long antedated the crisis itself. Contemporaries, however, had difficulty figuring out where one section began and the other ended, even after the Confederate states seceded. This indeterminacy of regional identities was, of course, much more pronounced in previous decades, when other, equally ill-defined regions, most notably the trans-Appalachian "West," jockeyed for relative advantage in the national political arena. In other words, *regionalism,* a sense of common interest and identity across an extended, if indeterminate, space, was a function of unpredictably changing circumstances and bears only a contingent relationship to the *regions* that scholars construct in order to organize and interpret a vast universe of historical data.

To think historically about regionalism, we have to explore this relationship between the "imagined communities" that ideologues conjured into existence and the complex social and cultural conditions they confronted.[6] Nationalists do not work on blank slates: they must reconcile, reorient, or replace preexisting loyalties. It took years of political education and military mobilization for the

American colonists to convince themselves that they constituted an independent "people" and that this new identity was compatible with diverse definitions of fundamental rights and vital interests. Local and regional differences were not submerged in nationhood, but as they were brought forward—into consciousness and into the process of nation-building—they were transformed.

A new history of regionalism in the United States might begin with the creation of the new nation, and only then look backward toward the first colonial settlements. Consciousness of difference, the identification of economic interests or of cultural patterns that could divide Americans along regional lines, depended on a common context that had not existed before the Revolutionary conflict. Nationalism came first and was the necessary precondition for the development of regional consciousness. Regionalism was itself compatible with, and expressive of, Americans' sense of their national identity.[7] As South Carolina novelist William Gilmore Simms wrote, "To be *national* in literature, one must needs be *sectional*."[8] The original federal union did not collapse because Americans lacked a sufficiently developed sense of national identity to resist the seductive charms of sectionalist appeals. To the contrary, it was the precocious development of a collective, national identity during the protracted Revolutionary crisis that constituted the essential precondition for regional consciousness and the ultimate emergence of claims to new nationhood in the fire-eating South.

The history of American regional identities cannot be extricated from the development of American nationalism. Most Americans through most of their history would deny that there is any tension, much less fundamental incompatibility, between these collective identities or that they should be distinguished from one another in the first place. To understand how this could be so, we have to return to the time of the new nation's founding. The intention here is not to call the success of the founders into question (though of course the Civil War does so) but rather to explore the ways in which Americans imagined themselves to be a people and how these ideas were shaped by the vast spaces of the extended republic. The new federal regime yoked regional consciousness to national identity. From its founding, the new nation was a nation of regions.

1 • Federalism, Republicanism, and the Origins of American Sectionalism

Peter S. Onuf

The sectional crisis that destroyed the union in 1861 resulted from the failure of national political institutions, including, finally and most tellingly, the political parties. Bonds of union weakened as sectional differences became more pronounced and intractable; sectionalism, the growing awareness of fundamental and irreconcilable difference, could no longer be contained by an increasingly brittle and unresponsive national political system. This conventional view is plausible, even compelling. But it would be a mistake to view sectionalism as an exogenous factor, distinct from the political system itself.

In constructing sectionalist mythologies, Southerners and Northerners discovered the origins of their respective "civilizations" in distinctive historical experiences; they agreed that separate development was a function of the fundamental commitment to slave or free labor. Yet the most powerful explanation for sectional difference was to be found in the divergent moral development of Northerners and Southerners. Such explanations came easily to the heirs of republican Revolutionaries, accustomed as they were to projecting conspiratorial designs onto their corrupt foes; antebellum sentimentalists reinforced republican paranoia by linking bad politics to a comprehensive, multifaceted depravity. Critics of the South focused relentlessly on violations of "family values," and defenders returned the favor. Sectionalism was thus *essentialized*, conceived as an autonomous force that would periodically erupt on the national scene, by being located in the character of individuals shaped by distinctive social systems.[1]

The premise of this essay is that, contrary to contemporary and contemporaneous mythologies about what precipitated the final rupture of the union, sectional conflict was not a function of fundamentally different social systems or civilizations, or of the distinctive morality or character of Southerners and Northerners, but was instead integral to the original conception and construction of the federal system. This does not mean that the union was somehow fated to collapse, regardless of what subsequent generations made of it. But the conceptual framework for articulating sectional differences was developed by the founders. The paradoxical effect of subsequent efforts to sustain their union was to draw attention and give additional force to its sectional antithesis.

Sectionalism and union were inextricably linked in the creation of the federal republic. Federalist proponents of a more powerful national government emphasized the dangers of emerging sectional distinctions: the collapse of the union would lead to the formation of separate, potentially hostile regional unions. The reformers' sectionalist scenarios helped secure the establishment of a more "respectable" and "energetic" central government in 1789. But they also developed the script for sectional conflict. Federalist proponents of the Constitution juxtaposed the promise of growing harmony and interdependence against the awful possibility of disunion. Unionist rhetoric was thus shadowed by the immanent threat of sectional strife; efforts to secure the union constituted an ultimately self-fulfilling prophecy of disunion.

Nationalism and Sectionalism

In defending provincial liberties against the pretensions of central authority, American Revolutionaries closely conformed to the model of revolutionary or restorationist movements throughout early modern Europe.[2] But the logic of American resistance transcended the grievances of frustrated or displaced provincial elites. Under conditions of broadening popular political activity and rising expectations, the claims of the provincial periphery were dissoci-

ated from the social structure of the colonial old regime. The association between an expanding periphery and the democratization of
political and social life constituted the crucial, distinctively modern
dimension of the American Revolutionary movement. Nationalism
in America developed in tandem with opposition to centralized
state power; sectionalism was its logical corollary.[3]

A republican scheme of representation guaranteed that neither
center nor periphery would be fixed, thus precluding the invidious,
unequal, and exploitative relations among specific places that constituted the antitype of American nationality.[4] In contrast to its
early modern predecessors, the American Revolution did not promote the interests of particular localities and their traditional ruling
elites, but rather those of localities generally and their popularly
chosen representatives. A broadly appealing conception of American nationhood thus depended on preempting concentrations of
aristocratic power on a static provincial periphery as well as pre-
venting the development of a domineering metropolis.[5]

Both before and after independence, vigilant republicans sought
to guard against dangerous concentrations of power. Given a
widely dispersed population and the absence of deep, legally sanctioned social distinctions among free whites, it is hardly surprising
that these fears should be conceptualized in spatial, geographical
terms. Radical republican assaults on the monarchical and aristocratic tendencies of their allegedly counterrevolutionary opponents
played on pervasive popular anxieties about the political and economic domination of one *place* or region over another. In other
words, the political sociology of British radical Whigs, focused on
the "corruption" of a benign social order, gave way under American circumstances to the political geography of Revolutionary republicans: the analytical axis flipped from vertical to horizontal.

But why should Americans continue to fear the domination of a
powerful metropolis after independence? It was not simply a case
of paranoid projection, belied in fact by the retarded development
of the "federal village" at Washington, D.C. Americans had always
worried about the relative advantages and disadvantages of their
localities; and they were intensely aware that favored places often
gained and secured their advantages through political means. Fears
of comparative geographical disadvantage were exacerbated by the

collapse of imperial authority. As they constituted a new national government, the founding generation became increasingly conscious of the distinctive interests of different places. Controversial policy issues inevitably raised questions about the relative situation and future prospects of states and regions.

The new federal system guaranteed that the new nation's political geography would remain in a state of constant flux. Recoiling from British tyranny, Americans sought to preempt the emergence of a dominant capital or favored metropolitan region; curbs on the center were matched by the empowerment of an expanding periphery, as new states were added to the union. A dynamic political geography reinforced the American tendency to think spatially about national identity and about their own place in the nation. The genius of the American people, patriots proclaimed, was to conquer space, to transcend distances and differences across the continent. But by providing a context and language for identifying regional identities and interests, conceiving American nationality in such expansive terms also inevitably heightened sectional consciousness.

The transformation of British imperial patriotism into American nationalism pivoted on a radical reconception of the role of the center in American politics.[6] Popular sovereignty, the legitimating fiction of patriotic resistance and national identity, was conceptualized in terms of the equal representation of places and of the self-governing citizens who lived there but who might in time move on to other places.[7] The demystification of metropolitan authority and the empowerment of the provincial periphery were most conspicuous in the movement to relocate capitals at the geographical centers of the states and to fix the new national capital at the center of the union.[8] Equal rights in these new republican regimes required equal access to the centers of power. The federal system thus promoted a sense of national identity not by eliminating or emasculating the states, but rather by facilitating free movement among them, by guaranteeing that no state or states would enjoy an artificial preponderance of power, and by providing for the formation of new states as settlement spread across the hinterland.[9]

Nationalism is a pathway to political modernity, because it facilitates the unimpeded movement of people and resources across the extended but bounded space that a "people" occupies and exploits.[10] Under American conditions, national identity depended, not on dissolving preexisting parts in an homogenous whole, but rather on rationalizing, generalizing, and equalizing the claims of constituent parts—beginning with the irreducible claims of sovereign citizens—in an expansively inclusive, homogenizing whole.[11] Boundaries were not erased but made permeable. Respect for the equal rights of separate, sovereign states was the only security for sustaining the union, the sine qua non of American nationhood.

The emergence of sectionalism in antebellum America was predicated on the pervasiveness of nationalist sentiment, not on its absence or retarded development. American nationalism flourished without a great metropolis, a privileged central place that attracted and absorbed provincial wealth and talent. Distance from the center thus was not, as it had been for colonial Americans, a measure of diminishing power and influence in a hierarchy of particular places; instead, all places were supposed to be or to become equal. Sectional consciousness emerged out of pervasive anxieties that this fundamental premise would be betrayed, that selfish politicians would promote the parochial concerns of one region at the expense of others, that an unholy alliance of interest groups would construct a powerful central government that would enable favored regions to extend their rule across the continent.

Federalists and Antifederalists

In the 1780s many anxious observers feared that the American experiment in republican government would fail. An increasingly fragile and tenuous union seemed likely to collapse; when it did, distinctive and potentially hostile regional interests would find expression in new governments that would confront one another in a "state of nature."[12] The western lands controversy, one of the leading sources of conflict in the Confederation years, would be reopened on a much wider, more violent scale as the disunited states competed for control of the vast, undeveloped hinterland. Here was "an ample theatre for hostile pretensions," Alexander Hamilton wrote in *The Federalist*, no. 7, as were "competitions of commerce"; "the public debt of the Union would be a further cause

16 • Peter S. Onuf

of collision between the separate States or confederacies."[13] During the Constitutional Convention, James Madison projected the starkest, most prescient division, between states that relied on slavery and those that did not: "the great danger to our general government *is the great southern and northern interests of the continent, being opposed to each other.*"[14]

Constitutional reformers argued that divisions along sectional lines would play into the hands of, if they were not actually fomented by, the new nation's counterrevolutionary imperial neighbors. Unrestrained regional rivalries would destroy the union; they would replicate "European" conditions in America and invite European interventions.[15] Yet the actual limits of these projected unions remained controversial. Would the Middle States constitute a separate union? If not, would Pennsylvania be aligned with the southern or "eastern" confederation? Far from being fixed, regional interests and identities were prospective, depending on political and diplomatic contingencies at home and abroad.

As the ratification debates so clearly reveal, Americans of the Revolutionary era were intensely conscious of the local and regional differences that threatened their continuing union. Opponents of the new Constitution were no less sensitive to these dangers than were its advocates. Antifederalists portrayed themselves as authentic Revolutionary patriots, predicting that the new regime would foster divisive and destructive regional rivalries.[16] They warned that the Constitution would exacerbate, not alleviate, the conflicts it was ostensibly designed to resolve. The imposition of central governmental control across the continent, a Pennsylvania Antifederalist predicted, would lead to "a civil war with all its dreadful train of evils."[17] The immediate danger was not Europeanization but rather a return to the conditions of imperial rule, when a distant metropolis exercised despotic power over weak and vulnerable American provinces. Nothing less than *"an iron-handed despotism . . .* could connect and govern these United States under one government," opponents of ratification in Pennsylvania insisted.[18]

Discounting the dangers of disunion, Antifederalists projected a radically different political geography than did their Federalist foes. A new American metropolis, the center of power and privilege, would dominate the periphery; the judicial and administrative apparatus of an "energetic" central government would reinforce this dominance as the new capital and its hinterland grew strong and prosperous at the expense of remote provinces. "The benefits of government would collect in the centre," predicted the "Federal Farmer" (probably Melancton Smith).[19] The inevitable result, "Agrippa" (James Winthrop) concluded, was that "the extremes of the empire" would be "drained to fatten an over-grown capital."[20]

Federalists and Antifederalists evoked alternative visions of the new nation's future prospects and of the ways in which the Revolution could be undone. These alternatives were conceptualized in spatial, geographic terms: for Federalists, the imminent danger was that emergent regions would take on a political form and confront one another as rival sovereignties; Antifederalists countered that just such a competition was already taking place and that ratification of the Constitution would secure the dominant position of one region or another.[21] Federalists warned that the disintegration of the union would lead to the Europeanization of American politics. Antifederalists countered that the proposed reform would recreate the conditions that had provoked revolution in the first place. A new national metropolis would exercise despotic authority over an oppressed provincial periphery.[22]

Polemicists on both sides in the ratification debate emphasized the advantages or disadvantages of the proposed system for their particular localities.[23] Such appeals were certainly effective, and they conjured up positive conceptions of regional interest. But Federalists and Antifederalists alike presented themselves as the true legatees of the Revolution and therefore as defenders of the American union as a whole. The rhetorical thrust on both sides was *unionist;* opponents were depicted as *disunionists* whose real, unacknowledged intention was to promote the interests of specific localities at the expense of others. Neither Federalists nor Antifederalists openly avowed sectional bias; rather, they imputed and projected sectionalist motives to their opponents. This is hardly surprising: in the context of a debate about the future of the union both sides would, of course, attempt to seize the high ground. The rhetorical and conceptual confusion engendered by this first crisis of union proved to be fertile ground for emerging sectional consciousness, for the construction of the conflicting political geographies that would ultimately destroy the union.

Original Intentions

The emergence of distinctive, potentially hostile sections in early American politics was by no means a foregone conclusion. History and common experience mitigated against sectionalism. The union of thirteen colonies had itself emerged as an increasingly self-conscious and aggrieved "section" on the British imperial periphery, and its claims remained compelling after independence.[24] The failure to negotiate a satisfactory peace settlement after the Revolution, most notably on the terms of Anglo-American trade, sustained a broader sense of a common cause and national interest even as the Confederation government tottered toward collapse. During the ratification debates, Federalists sought to mobilize nationalist sentiment by emphasizing the new nation's perilous international situation.[25] Antifederalists, presenting themselves as vigilant defenders of Revolutionary republicanism, challenged this analysis and questioned the Federalists' motives. But there was no ideological warrant or rhetorical space for avowed sectionalists in these debates. Proponents of sectional interests could not make plausible patriotic appeals that were grounded in a distinctive and exclusive shared experience or that pointed toward a unique sectional destiny.

Yet if Americans were reluctant to acknowledge a sectionalist agenda, they were well prepared to discover one in the conspiratorial machinations of opponents. During the ratification debates, Antifederalists sought to define—or uncover—the original intentions of the framers, thus setting the pattern for subsequent constitutional controversy. The paradoxical effect of attempting to fix fundamental principles in constitutional texts, where meanings would be unequivocal and intentions transparent, was to put a premium on the act of interpretation.[26] Antifederalists charged that framers did not necessarily mean what the proposed federal Constitution apparently said; whatever they meant, their ambiguous language provided openings for potentially dangerous constructions. Critics of the Constitution therefore pressed for the introduction of more precise formulations, in the form of amendments, that would preclude artful constructions that jeopardized individual liberties and state rights. But, as Madison noted in *The Federalist*, no. 37, achieving such textual closure was an illusory, self-subverting goal: "When the Almighty himself condescends to address mankind in their own language, his meaning, luminous as it must be, is rendered dim and doubtful, by the cloudy medium through which it is communicated."[27] Accordingly, the Antifederalists' great contribution to American jurisprudence was not so much the series of amendments that Madison pushed through the first Congress as it was a critical skepticism about words and deeds, text and intentions, that underscored the importance of constitutional interpretation. Divergent constructions of the Constitution in turn provided justificatory language for unselfconscious sectionalists who persisted in proclaiming their devotion to the union.

Both sides in the ratification controversy contributed to the emergence of antebellum sectionalism. Latter-day sectionalists characteristically represented themselves as authentic unionists and true defenders of the Federalists' Constitution. Their solicitude for regional interest was framed in defensive and principled terms. Threats to the union came from other sections, which were all too prone to seize and abuse federal power, never from the defensive stratagems of the victimized region. This perennial concern about the dangerous concentration of power in a new imperial center was the most conspicuous legacy of Antifederalist republicanism for sectionalist thought.

Sectionalism flourished in early national politics because it was never acknowledged as such but was instead projected onto others who, heedless of the Revolutionaries' precious legacy, were bent on destroying the union. It was easier for American statesmen to characterize their opponents as sectionalists than to acknowledge such impulses in themselves. Revolutionary republicanism taught them to think in conspiratorial terms, to be on the lookout for secret enemies who would sacrifice the general good for particular advantage.[28] Antifederalist vigilance against constitutional encroachments thus offered the best security for the Federalists' great achievement, the "more perfect union" that supposedly harmonized conflicting sectional interests.[29] The ironic result of this con-

ception of the union was to validate increasingly expansive definitions of distinctive regional interests that were ultimately incom-
patible with the union's continued existence.

Sectionally distinctive and divisive conceptions of American nationality became increasingly salient precisely because sections as
such have no formal standing in the federal Constitutional text.
This is not to say that concerns for sectional interests were not
prominent, even preeminent, at the Philadelphia Convention.[30]
The disjunction between a text that was devoted to balancing and
accommodating state and central governmental powers and the
prevailing sense that the real issues before the Convention had to
do with how those powers would be deployed provided fertile
ground for sectionalist thought. It is hardly surprising that the delegates' endorsement of a strong central government would be contingent on calculations about the impact of its power on the interests of their constituents, most notably in negotiating treaties and
regulating commerce. The history of the Confederation showed
that bare majorities would not hesitate to exploit their temporary
advantage, with potentially disastrous effects for the losers. Awareness of this danger constitutes the best simple explanation for the
Confederation's legendary "imbecility." A jealous regard for states'
rights did not proceed from a naive belief in the self-sufficiency of
the new state-republics, but rather from a widespread agreement
that the power of the Confederation Congress was so vulnerable to
abuse, a danger that generally was conceptualized in sectional
terms.[31]

The challenge to the Philadelphia Convention was to limit and
complicate the exercise of the central government's powers in ways
that would prevent evanescent sectional voting blocs from gaining
undue and dangerous advantage. Of course, the great majority of
delegates were "nationalists" who favored a significant, substantive expansion of central governmental power. But every delegate
understood that different schemes for organizing and exercising
that central power would affect local and regional interests differ-
ently and that disunion might be preferable to a system too heavily
weighted toward adverse interests.

The founders had to secure sectional interests without drawing
attention to them. Early in the Convention Edmund Randolph pro-

posed a triple executive representing three distinct regions; later on, Gouverneur Morris urged that the original, Eastern states be given a permanent Constitutional veto over proliferating new states in the West.[32] Delegates rejected both proposals, recognizing that they would impose a dangerous rigidity and inflexibility on the new system. Shifts in population and wealth would create a new balance of power in the union; there was no way to anticipate the ultimate limits and alignments of sectional blocs that were already difficult to define. Equally importantly, delegates knew that explicit concessions to specific sectional interests would jeopardize ratification in other parts of the country.

Yet, as both friends and opponents of ratification understood, the proposed Constitution was the product of protracted intersectional negotiation and compromise. According to the Federalists, the founders' success in accommodating these disparate and potentially hostile interests was "miraculous."[33] Federalist rhetoric thus exaggerated the sectionalist and disunionist impulses of the Confederation in order to justify the concentration of power in the new federal regime. Unlike the Confederation Congress, the new government could never be dominated by one group of states at the expense of the others. Antifederalists were bound to argue the opposite: that the much maligned Confederation offered ample security for the rights and interests of its members and that the consolidation of power in the new central government would precipitate a fatal contest for sectional advantage.[34] If in the Federalists' account sectionalism would be superseded by a more perfect union under the new Constitution, their Antifederalist opponents reversed the terms: union would give way to civil convulsions, the states would be destroyed, and one section—a new imperial center—would give rule to subject provinces.

The ratification debates revolved around alternative *sectionalisms*, imaginary political geographies that enabled antagonists to conceptualize dangers to and prospects for the American union. Union and section were thus inextricably paired: it was impossible to think or talk about one without suggesting the other. Of course, sectional alignments could not exist in the first place without a *national* political arena. Sectional consciousness was thus a topdown phenomenon, the result of ad hoc alliances among state

leaders who discovered common interests as they sought to promote or obstruct the exercise of central governmental power.

Sections and Interests: Virginia and New England

Americans were well aware of pervasive cultural differences and
conflicts of interest among the far-flung regions that constituted
their union. These differences were exaggerated and exacerbated
by the unprecedented risks and opportunities of the new national
political arena and the volatile status of foreign commercial relations. Under these novel and unpredictable circumstances, attachment to local interest did not translate into consciousness of fixed
and durable regional identities. No one could accurately predict
the contingencies that would shape future alliances. The Virginians
who took a leading role in the national constitutional reform
movement were particularly poor prophets.

Visionary Virginians believed that the shift from tobacco to
wheat in the Chesapeake region pointed toward new geopolitical
alignments. Improved transportation would facilitate trade with an
expanding economic hinterland in the Ohio Valley, creating new
opportunities for economic diversification and development.[35] The
economies of Virginia and Maryland would become more like
Pennsylvania's. Though rivals for relative advantage in the Ohio
country, these three states and their neighbors would eventually
constitute a regional bloc in Congress. Flourishing trade ties would
draw the rising new states in the West into their orbit.

Solicitude for narrowly defined local interests had to be balanced
against the practical political imperatives of alliance-building. A
state's effective power in Congress and therefore its political and
economic future depended on augmenting the ranks of like-
minded voters, and this in turn depended on expansive definitions
of common interest. The resulting alignments might be described
as sectional blocs, but this was not a sectionalism that proceeded
from consciousness of fixed, essential differences. American statesmen sought to suppress and minimize differences in order to extend their influence as widely as possible. From this perspective,
the nationalist impulse was indistinguishable from the sectionalist:

both represented imaginative efforts to conceive and promote collective, translocal interests.[36]

Given their primarily agricultural economies, it is not surprising that state leaders would look for allies to neighboring states with similar crops and therefore similar interests in the Atlantic economy. Virginia's central location, ultimately ratified by the siting of the new national capital, meant that it could promote political and economic ties in all directions. The first task was to overcome a history of acrimonious jurisdictional conflicts with Maryland over Potomac navigation and development of ungranted western lands. Resolution of these disputes set the stage for a new regional condominium, including Pennsylvania, that would promote beneficial commercial regulations. Recognizing that the Confederation presented formidable political and constitutional obstacles to these ambitions, forward-looking regionalists sought to draw more distant states into new accords on commerce and ultimately into drafting a new federal charter.

Madison and other patriotic Virginians could construct progressively more expansive and inclusive imaginary political geographies, extending far beyond their own boundaries—which were in any case indeterminate—and beyond putatively natural alliances with their immediate neighbors.[37] They had no difficulty in identifying, or confusing, the interests and prospects of their "country" Virginia with those of the union as a whole. There was no compelling reason to split the difference, as later generations of Southern nationalists would do, and link the history and destiny of Virginia to that of a particular section.

Revolutionary Virginians rewrote the history of the Old Dominion in order to buttress their state's claims to a central position in the new federal republic. This "intellectual reconstruction" worked against sectional consciousness.[38] Virginia came into its own, according to its historians, as it assumed the leading role in *continental* resistance to British tyranny; Virginia's leadership was predicated on a broad Revolutionary consensus and on the willingness of patriotic Americans from all the colonies to be led. A tradition of reformist writing in the pre-Revolutionary years prepared the way for strictures against racial slavery in the new histories of the commonwealth.[39] By minimizing differences between Virginia and emergent "free" states to the north, antislavery talk also served a vitally important purpose in promoting the new state's hegemonic ambitions. Slavery was seen as historically contingent, an unfortunate consequence of the old regime: it did not define Virginia. Most white Virginians, historian John Daly Burk insisted, saw slavery as "an evil of the most serious and afflicting nature" and were prepared to seek a "remedy, whenever it shall appear safe or practicable."[40] For progressive Virginians, the notion that states that relied heavily on slave labor should form an alliance dedicated to the institution's perpetuation was anathema.[41] Of course, to skeptical contemporaries and subsequent historians, this is precisely what the new union was: a craven capitulation to slaveholding interests, or what William Lloyd Garrison would call a "covenant with death."[42]

The most skeptical critics of Virginian pretensions, those most likely to detect a latent proslavery, sectionalist intent in the federal Constitution, were New Englanders. But New Englanders were equally, perhaps even more, vulnerable to charges that they were sectionalists. New England was by far the most self-consciously distinctive region in the country, its delegates to Congress most likely to act in concert with one another. But New England leaders recognized that this distinctiveness—the appearance of taking a forward role in the patriot coalition in order to serve their constituents' particular interests—constituted a potentially fatal liability to the common cause. The famous alliance between radicals in Massachusetts and Virginia was a calculated effort to minimize the risk that intersectional suspicions directed at the one sectional bloc with a history of common action in pursuit of common interests would abort the revolutionary movement.

Sectional consciousness among New Englanders was not simply a function of common historical experiences. According to the logic of Confederation politics, alliance-building was most problematic at the extremes of the union. Where ambitious Virginians could expand their influence to the north and west, New Englanders could only turn to one another. While the northern frontiers offered some opportunities for speculation and development, large numbers of ambitious New Englanders moved west, and out of their natal states' political orbit.

The dangers of depopulation, impoverishment, and a marginalized position in the Confederation inspired widespread antiexpansionist sentiment in the Northeast.[43] Slavery did not loom large in these fearful calculations; after all, slaves were held in every New England state in 1776. The concern instead was with a shifting regional balance of power, a concern predicated on the sense that New England *was* a region and that its opportunities for extending its influence or even sustaining its present position in the union were radically limited.

New Englanders were the most sectionally conscious Revolutionaries but were forced to suppress and deny their distinctiveness as they sought crucial support from other parts of the country. The dynamic of congressional politics worked against New Englanders, however, making them increasingly conscious of their relative disadvantages and therefore of their common sectional interests. Many New Englanders thus would become enthusiastic nationalists, hoping for a new regime that would promote interests that had been systematically frustrated under the Confederation. Yet, as precocious sectionalists, New Englanders would also prove the most receptive to separatist appeals. During the "critical period," proposals for a separate confederation in New England were uniquely and uncharacteristically substantive. "It is . . . now time to form a new and stronger union," read a proposal from early 1787 urging creation of "a new Congress, as the Representative of the nation of New-England." No other group of states was well enough defined or had had the common historical experiences or consciousness of distinct regional interests to be confused with a "nation."[44]

The new federal Constitution preempted the threat of New England separatism (for the time being) by giving the new Congress authority over interstate and foreign trade. The demand for national commercial regulation was general, as the national constitutional reform movement had shown, but had been thwarted by the ability of any single state to veto any amendment to the Articles of Confederation. It was therefore easy for Federalist proponents of ratification to identify New Englanders' interests with the national interest and to promise that they would benefit from a developing and dynamic "union of interests." The region would no longer find itself at a relative disadvantage, at the margins of the union, as it sought to gain allies and extend its influence. New England merchants would be leading beneficiaries of a stable free trade regime at home and the negotiation of more favorable terms of trade with foreign powers. At the same time, rapid development of the national domain promised extraordinary opportunities to Yankee speculators, entrepreneurs, and settlers.

Development-minded nationalists envisioned a new, more perfect union that would dissolve and transcend emergent sectional distinctions. Though the tendency of Confederation politics might be for mutually exclusive interests to coalesce along regional lines, nationalists insisted that this was by no means a natural or inevitable outcome. An energetic but constitutionally limited central government that would secure state rights and civil liberties offered optimal conditions for what Madison later called a true "consolidation" of "interests and affections" across the continent.[45] According to this account, the pursuit of interest could be a source of strength for union, perhaps even its fundamental ground. "Under a wise government," a New Yorker wrote in 1790, the apparent "diversity" of interests across the continent "will prove the cement of the union."[46]

The Federalists' most crucial rhetorical move was to dissociate *section* and *interest*. Though the Confederation fostered state "jealousy" and an exaggerated, divisive solicitude for sectional interests, proponents of the new federal Constitution argued that the natural tendency of interest was toward union. But this formulation could cut both ways. In order to make the reconstruction of the union seem imperative, Federalists warned that section and interest would converge and the union would collapse if their campaign for a stronger central government failed. By this logic, later generations of politicians could interpret any line of policy that seemed to result in systematic sectional disadvantage as evidence that their opponents were conspiring against the union. The Federalists of 1787–88 authorized a powerful, negative link between union and section that would come back to haunt their successors.

Federalists asserted that union was contingent: if the federal government were not given extensive new powers, the union would disintegrate. Market relations and transportation links constituted another crucial contingency. The pursuit of interest could only sustain union where mutually beneficial exchange was possible. Union might be "natural," but nature would take a different course if the central government failed to regulate the distribution of public lands, sponsor internal improvements, or extend American jurisdiction over river systems and their ports. The Federalists' notion of a contingent and therefore consciously constructed union was predicated on their perception of the fluidity and dynamism of interdependent economic interests. An expanding union would provide ample scope for a developing "consolidation" of interests; it would also undermine any essentialist account of sectional differences. Sectional alignments in the Confederation Congress were at best imprecisely defined, and then only in response to the diplomatic and commercial crises of the mid-1780s. The addition of new states would make the limits of these "sections" even more a function of opportunistic, shifting, ad hoc alliances. The more inclusive such alliances became, the more diverse, and therefore incoherent, the range of interests they would represent and promote.

The Rise and Fall of the West

The artificiality of sectionalism under the dynamic conditions of the early republic—the sense that there were no fixed, essential connections between particular people, places, and interests—was most apparent in the rapid development of the Ohio Valley. Settlers in this region were the first self-conscious, avowed sectionalists in American history. What was distinctive about these Westerners, or so they claimed, was that they had shed the habits and prejudices of their natal states. "Take the Virginian from his plantation, or the Yankee from his boat and harpoon, or from his snug cottage" and settle him in the West, asserted Cincinnati editor James Hall, and each would soon become "a different man; his *national character* will burst the chains of local habit."[47] Westerners, including settlers on both sides of the Ohio, and beyond, portrayed themselves as quintessential *Americans,* and their "section" as a place where sectional distinctions were resolved and transcended. In this self-congratulatory rhetoric, sectional identity merged with a vaulting sense of the nation's glorious future and a patriotic devotion to the union.[48]

These patriotic effusions can be seen as yet another chapter in the history of American boosterism, as local publicists sought to attract settlers and investment from all parts of the country and from abroad. Yet minimizing differences among Westerners themselves, differences that would become increasingly conspicuous as controversy over the future of slavery in the territories polarized American politics, meant that Western polemicists would emphasize and exaggerate sectional distinctions elsewhere. Thus, just as Western boosters were the most authentic legatees of the Federalists' expansive, developmental rhetoric, they also emphasized the reality, if only implicitly the dangers, of sectional differences. Union and section thus were inextricably linked: positively, as boosters identified the West with the nation's destiny; negatively, as they juxtaposed the harmony of interests that supposedly characterized their bustling region with the conflicts and jealousies of mutually antagonistic sections in the East.

The sense of contingency, that union depended on an energetic federal government that would act decisively to promote expansion and development, was pronounced in Western rhetoric, as it had been in Federalist warnings about the dangers of disunion. The Louisiana crisis in 1802–3 inspired an outburst of nationalist sentiment in the West. The loyalties of the Jeffersonian Republicans who dominated political life in the Western states and territories could hardly be doubted. "No consideration on earth would induce them to attach themselves to any other power on earth," James Jackson of Georgia assured the Senate in February 1803.[49] But senators well understood that a powerful French presence at New Orleans capable of interdicting American trade down the Mississippi could easily destroy the union. Celebrations of the Louisiana Purchase betrayed a sense of dangers narrowly averted. A crisis as momentous and fraught with danger as the constitutional crisis of the 1780s had been suddenly, almost miraculously resolved, as the new nation stood poised at the brink of sectional conflict, civil war, foreign intervention, Native American attack, and slave revolts.[50]

The Burr Conspiracy, of 1804–7, again raised questions about Western loyalties, but the elimination of a credible foreign threat to the west and south limited the diplomatic options of would-be separatists.[51] Westerners instead mobilized their political power in Congress to promote their interests, insisting that the union's future prosperity and power depended on the federal government's responsiveness to regional needs. Their demands—for the creation of new states that would give them an effective voice in national politics, the rapid distribution of public lands, a vigorous program of public works and internal improvements, and outlets for agricultural surpluses—established the broad framework for intersectional political negotiations. Western politicians quickly grasped the opportunities for promoting their agenda by exploiting divisions among their Eastern counterparts.[52] Sectionalism in the East thus offered Westerners political leverage while reinforcing their own satisfying sense of having transcended such invidious, particularistic distinctions.

The "West" did not always represent a cohesive sectional bloc in national politics, for the boundaries of this emergent region were constantly shifting. Once the national domain was transferred to private hands, long-settled states like Ohio were less interested in low prices and easy terms and more interested in sustaining the revenue yield from public land sales. Westerners might rally behind a comprehensive federal program of internal improvements, but the successful initiation of improvement programs on the state level (Ohio is again the most conspicuous case) could undercut the urgency of the issue.[53] In prospect, improvements would "bind the union together"; the reality was far more complicated. Not only did the siting of turnpikes, canals, and later railroads have a decisive impact on local development prospects, it also directed flows of goods and capital into increasingly well defined regional and interregional patterns.[54]

The articulation of economically distinctive regions was a function of the rapid expansion of the national economy. Internal improvements may have strengthened the union, as visionary political economists of the founding period had anticipated and as Henry Clay and other improvers continued to argue, but they also prefigured the regional distinctions that would lead to the union's collapse. Clay, the great compromiser and unionist, portrayed his American System as an antidote to the sectional differences fostered by the debate over slavery. The distinctive political economies and legal regimes in states where slavery was eliminated or entrenched were particularly conspicuous and troubling to Clay and other border state politicians. For these union-minded regionalists, the Ohio River was the central artery of a dynamic, interdependent political economy, a section to transcend and ultimately absorb all other sections. Their central premise was that Eastern differences would be resolved in Western development. Sectional divisions over slavery, projected westward with increasingly acrimonious debate over the future of slavery in the territories and new states, thus constituted a fundamental challenge to Western unionists.[55]

The failure of gradual emancipation schemes, which enjoyed wide support in Clay's Kentucky, and abolitionist assaults on the social and moral orders of the slave states forged an increasingly powerful link between section and interest. Union, Clay understood, could not be taken for granted. A willingness to compromise was essential but not in itself sufficient; what was needed was an exercise of political will, a commitment to constructing a national political economy that promoted harmonious, interdependent development. The alternative, the "natural" result of a failure of will, was the rise of increasingly autonomous and hostile sectional blocs.

In the decades leading up to the Civil War it became increasingly difficult for Clay and other Westerners to sustain their cherished belief that they had moved beyond invidious sectional distinctions. Western sectionalism, the notion that Western society embodied the American future, was the casualty of a new kind of sectionalism. In reciprocal ways, Northern and Southern sectional consciousness was predicated on a growing awareness of *essential* differences. These differences were made manifest in the construction of radically contradictory histories of accumulating grievances, articulated in and validated by the language of the Revolutionary forefathers.

Parties and Sections

Republican ideology provided the medium for articulating fundamental, irreconcilable sectional differences and for reducing a dynamic, fractured regional landscape to the single great division between North and South. Republicanism could play this role because it was simultaneously the language of nationalism, the patriotic idiom of the Revolutionary fathers.[56] Nationalists became sectionalists, or so they told themselves, only because of their continuing fealty to the principles of the Revolution, because their antagonists had seized control of the national government in order to promote their own selfish, sectional agenda. The warnings of skeptical Antifederalists now seemed increasingly prophetic.

The dialectical relationship between union and section was first forged in the debate over the ratification of the federal Constitution. The link was further strengthened by the ascendancy of the Jeffersonian Republicans, the first great popular political party, who coalesced around opposition to the "consolidationist" tendencies of the Hamiltonians, who dominated the new federal government. Denying that they constituted a party dedicated to promoting particular interests, sectional or otherwise, Republicans projected factious or partisan intentions onto defenders of the administration. But it was only in the dark days of the late 1790s, with Federalists riding the quasi-war with France to new heights of popularity, that the Republicans developed a winning formula. In promoting the "principles of 1798" Republicans presented themselves as the true defenders of *union:* the Federalists jeopardized union because they sought to advance *sectional* interests. Jefferson's Revolution of 1800 was a vindication and restoration of a union that was predicated on civil liberties and states' rights.[57]

In their original incarnation, the Republicans constituted the sort of antipartisan party that Revolutionary republicanism sanctioned. Not surprisingly, they fashioned a critique of Hamiltonian consolidationism that played on the fears of a domineering metropolis that had moved provincial Americans to assert their independence and that had inspired Antifederalist opposition to the Constitution during the ratification controversy. But the failure to check Federalist power at the national level, signified by passage of the Alien and Sedition Acts (1798), dictated a political—and ideological—retreat to the states. As Jefferson and Madison articulated the federal relationship in the Kentucky and Virginia resolutions, the threat of consolidationism seemed as much a question of illegitimate sectional power as one of a despotic central government. The Republicans thus fashioned a conception of union secured by the constitutional exercise of states' rights and proof against the sectional bias now so apparent in the administration party.[58]

By depicting Federalists as sectionalists and linking their states' rights claims with true unionism, the ascendant Republicans could identify themselves with the framers of the federal Constitution. "We are all republicans, we are all federalists," Jefferson claimed in his first inaugural. "Let us, then, with courage and confidence pursue our own federal and republican principles, our attachment to our union and representative government."[59] In the future, the most conspicuous enemies of federal republicanism would not be the centralizing "monocrats" who had been routed from office by Jefferson's election. Far more plausible and insidious were those whose "attachment" to the union was most suspect, the sectionalists who would look beyond the union for succor and support once they lost control of the federal government.

The dispassionate modern observer might wonder at the Jeffersonian Republicans' logic. These self-proclaimed unionists did not hesitate to threaten disunion; they charged their opponents with being sectionalists at a time when they had retreated to their own sectional political base. Yet it is precisely under such conditions that denial and projection would be so crucial, when it was so necessary to convince themselves, as well as others, that they were acting in accord with the fundamental principles of the regime. Furthermore, the elaboration of this Jeffersonian vision was a blueprint for a broad-based political mobilization that would transcend sectionalist appeals. In taking the attack to the bastions of Federalist strength, Republicans would present themselves as the party of union and their opponents as the party of entrenched privilege and divisive local interest.

Scholarly understanding of Antifederalism and Jeffersonian Republicanism has been colored by the subsequent history of the states' rights debate and sectional conflict. Hostility to central power is identified with agrarianism, localism, and resistance to modernity. But Jefferson and his followers saw themselves as cosmopolitan progressives; they insisted that a durable union depended on obliterating the invidious distinctions that Federalism fostered. From their perspective, the Federalists' projection of a strong central state represented the counterrevolutionary antithesis of American nationality, the return to imperial rule and colonial dependency.[60]

The Republicans established the precedent for subsequent national political parties, fusing sectionalist charges against adversaries and patriotic encomiums to "federal and republican principles" with platforms that promised substantial benefits for all Americans. Yet the effect of such rhetoric was to draw attention to sectional differences, even as polemicists who evoked the shades of the the founding fathers promised that their party's programs would resolve and transcend them. At the same time, the informal conventions of national political life that were codified at recurrent moments of crisis in procedural rules and more or less explicit compromises suppressed discussion of divisive, sectional issues. These crises, most notably those of 1819–21, 1832–33, and 1850, prompted heroic efforts by latter-day compromisers to reenact and secure the great compromises of 1787 that had created the union.[61] The framers' dialectic, union against section, was thus reaffirmed and strengthened; but so too was the growing sense that the federal charter was shaped by specific and increasingly problematic intersectional accords that were no longer adequate to contemporary exigencies.

Suspicious that one section or other had gained disproportionate advantage at the outset or had subsequently succeeded in gaining control of the federal government to promote its own particular interests, compromisers and anticompromisers alike saw sectionalism everywhere. If unionism was ultimately drained of its ideological, symbolic, and moral content, it was because sectionalism ceased to be merely the antitype of union—the negative referent—and instead became its constitutive and defining term. If the point of union was simply intersectional accord, and this was the inevitable inference of successive compromises, then union was a contingent, instrumental good, the means to an end. Thinking of union in such terms, Northerners and Southerners might well question the costs of a continuing connection with people so essentially different from themselves.

As awareness of the importance of union faded, distinctive sectional interests grew increasingly salient, beginning with the Missouri crisis in 1819–21, Jefferson's "fire bell in the night . . . the knell of the Union."[62] These differences, suppressed, compromised, contested, become the main story line in American history through the Civil War, if not beyond. But the dangers of anachronism must be emphasized. However real these differences may seem to us, contemporaries were ill-equipped to grasp their fundamental, ultimately tragic implications. The conceptual paradigm for identifying or, perhaps more accurately, constructing distinctive, potentially hostile sections that could only be checked and transcended by an effective federal union seemed less and less compelling to the rising generation. In the founders' imaginary political geography, Europe was superimposed on America and intersectional conflicts of interest prefigured a state of war. That geography may now seem prophetic. But it proved to be prophetic only because it seemed so irrelevant to succeeding generations.

James Madison lived to see his countrymen forget why it had been so crucially important to save and strengthen the union in 1787. A shared sense of disaster averted—the collapse of the original Confederation into an anarchy of warring states or regional unions—was the strongest prop to union, the most compelling incentive for the "compromisers" who sustained it.[63] Madison, John Quincy Adams, Henry Clay, and Andrew Jackson were all "unionists" for whom the critical period of the 1780s, refracted through a second crisis of the union in 1807–14, was the primal, formative political experience. If subsequent generations of American politicians tended toward forgetfulness, it was not because they failed to revere the founders' achievement. It was instead the founders' apparent success, the absence of internal and external threats to the union by the mid-1820s, that made the concerns of the founders seem increasingly irrelevant.[64]

Abraham Lincoln complained in his famous Lyceum Address (1838) that young Americans did not face the ennobling challenges and opportunities that made their predecessors heroes.[65] With the end of European wars and entanglements, the elimination of security threats on the frontier, and the suppression of separatist movements, the union no longer seemed at risk. A more stable and less threatening international context also fostered a sense of American exceptionalism, the belief that the American states would never make war on one another, no matter how acrimonious their disputes, that they were somehow immune to the follies of the belligerent Old World. Madison and his fellow founders never embraced this providential, exceptionalist view of American history. Fixated on the near collapse of the American system in the 1780s and again in the War of 1812, they had no illusions about the American genius for peace and harmonious union. An effective commitment to union was predicated on consciousness of its fragility, a consciousness that fewer and fewer American statesmen shared after 1815.

Consciousness of sectional distinctions in the founding period reflected a selective and exaggerated interpretation of the conflicts that had threatened to immobilize the Confederation government. Pervasive anxieties about the future of the union underscored the dangers of unrestrained regional interest. By superimposing the image of Europe on the disintegrating Confederation, Madison and his fellow Federalists convinced themselves—and sought to convince skeptical voters—of the urgency of national constitutional reform. But because fewer and fewer Americans of later generations could imagine the Europeanization of American politics, they could not sustain the founders' sense of the dangers of sectionalism, even as "real" conflicts of increasingly rigid, distinctive, and self-conscious sectional interests multiplied apace.

The Madisonian conception of the union was superseded as fears of Europeanization subsided and the alternative imaginary geography conjured up in Antifederalist polemics—the domineering metropolis exploiting remote, victimized provinces—became increasingly salient.[66] Antebellum sectionalists adapted the vigilant, antipower ethos of Revolutionary republican resistance to imperial despotism to the new conditions of political competition in the federal republic.[67] "Republicanism" ultimately trumped "federalism," the founders' provision against disunion, Europeanization, and a return to the state of nature.

In a perverse, ironic reversal of the founding fathers' original formulation, for many Americans union was increasingly aligned with mere interest—a realm of prudence, calculation, and compromise (defined increasingly in our pejorative sense)—while sectionalism drew sustenance from deeper loyalties and more transcendent values. The national political parties destroyed the union by the steps they took to save it; their ultimate failure was inscribed in their short-term successes.[68] But in this, it should now be clear, they were following the lead of the framers themselves. For it was the framers who had first given life to the specter of sectional division and civil war as they sought to persuade skeptical voters to endorse their more energetic federal regime. Union may have been the founders' great legacy. But so was sectionalism, their great and tragic, self-fulfilling prophecy.

Differences to Die For

In retrospect, sectionalism may seem like—and function as—an imaginative pathway toward idealized local communities, the putative repositories of traditional American folkways and values. But antebellum politicians saw their world differently. The thrust of sectionalist alliance-building was integrative and nationalizing. To think in sectional terms was to look beyond specific localities, toward a more inclusive and therefore necessarily provisional and indeterminate conception of their own region and of the nation itself. The definition of sectional interest and identity constituted the necessary condition for imagining an inclusive national community within which all men, and all places, were created equal. Under American conditions, it was impossible *not* to think in sectional terms.

Yet if antebellum Americans were quick to see one another as sectionalists, they were reluctant to recognize particularistic impulses in themselves. This was not simply a case of self-deceiving obtuseness and the projection of corrupt motives onto unpatriotic others. Contemporaries could have no way of knowing that promoting or defending local and regional interests would ultimately lead to a crisis of union and national identity. Americans were taught to believe that the genius of republican government was to secure the rights and interests of localities as well as of individuals, the equality of places as well as of people. The promotion of a community's particular interests could be framed in the most general terms without a sense of dissonance or contradiction; the mobilization of citizens on a local or regional level could be represented as an effort to imagine and construct a more inclusive community of interest, the contingent approximation of a national idea that was itself boundless. Politicians could disavow a particularist, localist bias because Revolutionary republicanism universalized the particular and the local; political competition worked in the same direction, by rewarding politicians who could make the broadest possible appeal compatible with securing the interests of their constituents.

Nationalist sentiment in the antebellum United States was a protean force that would take increasingly distinctive and ultimately irreconcilable forms in different regions. The most crucial precipitant of this divergence was controversy over the extension of slavery. As the boundary between slave and free states became conspicuous, two great, well-defined sections subsumed the multiplicity of provisional, poorly defined sections and sectional alliances fostered by the proliferation of new states in the decentralized federal regime. Instead of competing for relative advantage within an expanding union, Southern slaveholders and Northern free-soilers sought to secure their vital interests by establishing the alignment of new states *before* they were admitted. A once boundless Western hinterland was thus imaginatively bounded.

The projection of South and North across the continent made those two great sections seem more distinct and therefore "real"; at the same time it challenged the status of the West itself as the section to end all sections, the place where the American promise would be fulfilled. The sphere of the nonnegotiable became progressively larger as the controversy over slavery deepened. Assuming defensive postures against putative encroachments on their rights, section-minded politicians increasingly interpreted the interests of their opponents in pejorative, ideological terms. Fealty to republican principles thus led sectionalists to essentialize sectional differences. To their amazement and horror, Americans discovered that these were differences worth dying for.

2 • New England as Region and Nation

Stephen Nissenbaum

The Elusive Region

New England would seem to be the perfect American region. Its history is long, and mostly it is proud. As early as 1614, even before the place was settled by Puritans, Captain John Smith gave New England its name, and his term quickly took hold. (Smith would never have thought to say that Virginia belonged to a place called "the South.") The corporation that settled Massachusetts in 1630 was initially named the New England Company, and by the 1680s the region had unwillingly achieved a sort of official recognition when King James II lumped its constituent colonies together—along with New York—and attempted without success to establish them as the collective Dominion of New England. New York has gone its separate way for some time now, but Vermont has been added to the list. For two centuries the boundaries of New England have been quite clearly defined: six contiguous states, five of them among the smallest in the nation. (Try to define the boundaries of "the South," or "the West," or any other region of the United States, and such precision withers away.) Even in terms of scale, New England is the tidiest of regions, conveying a sense of intimate villages and farms nestled among cragless hills, populated perhaps by America's "hobbits."

For a long time New England was the quintessential region of the United States. The term *Yankee* might refer to a New Englander, but, depending on one's perspective, it might also refer to a Northerner or simply to an American. As recently as 1938 Thornton Wilder was able to use the imaginary New Hampshire community of Grover's Corners as a symbol of the heart of the nation, giving it the universalized title *Our Town*.

But that has changed. It is difficult now to think of New England as America's heartland. Within the past few decades New England seems to have been replaced by a less precise entity known as "Middle America," a phrase redolent of both geographical centrality and ideological conservatism. (Even for liberals, Grover's Corners may have been replaced by *another* small town, imagined with a profound nostalgia distanced by an undercurrent of sophisticated irony: I am thinking of Garrison Keillor's Lake Woebegone.)

Meanwhile, within New England itself the pastoral heart of the region has been moving steadily north. In the eighteenth century "New England" was clearly moored in Connecticut, the "land of steady habits." By the mid-nineteenth century it had shifted to Massachusetts. Sometime early in the present century it began to migrate still further north, into Vermont, New Hampshire, and Maine. One hundred fifty years ago those states would have been dismissed as a land of half-civilized hillbillies; indeed, Al Capp was living in a small New Hampshire town when he created his imaginary Dogpatch.[1] But now that Connecticut is little more than a suburb of New York (the Connecticut Yankee being no more), and Massachusetts is a center of high-tech and academic culture, and those rural northern areas have become the last true bastion of the Yankee spirit—in effect, "New England's New England."

Let me broaden the issue. If the "real" New England has moved north, that fact is a direct consequence of the region's transformation. New England was the birthplace not only of the small town but also, arguably, of the industrial city. This is a crucial point. It was Gary Kulik who first pointed out to me that by 1860, when the New England small town was first being sentimentalized as a seat of pastoral Yankee stability, New England as a whole had become the single most urban part of the nation—the most industrial, the most Catholic, the most heavily immigrant in population, and the most rapidly changing area in the United States. Those facts have been largely ignored by New England regionalists. Or if not ignored, they have been marginalized, dutifully noted but not taken to be a defining element of the region's identity. Cities, factories, immigrants, Catholics—these may be present, but as New England's "other" face. That marginalization is surely one reason why the "real" New England has moved north. As Gary Kulik has noted, Thornton Wilder actually *does* refer to the presence of immigrants in Grover's Corners; at the very beginning of the play they are mentioned briefly—to be found on the *other* side of town. "Polish Town's across the tracks and some Canuck families," announces the narrator in his opening monologue. These immigrants play no role in the drama itself. Their absence suggests a tacit meaning of Wilder's title and makes it clear that the phrase "Our Town" is to be pronounced with the stress on the first word: "*Our* Town." Grover's Corners can be universalized only after it has first been purified.[2]

There is another problem. Well before small-town Yankee New England came to lose its imaginative hold as the spiritual heart of America, New England culture in a broader sense had become inextricably linked to the national culture. Even today students may study William Faulkner or William Gilmore Simms as Southern writers, or Willa Cather as a Midwesterner; but when it comes to Emerson, Thoreau, Hawthorne, Melville, and Dickinson, they are studying *American* literature. These New England writers defined the national cultural tradition. (That is even true for those who have been expelled from the unofficial canon: I am thinking of the poets Longfellow, Lowell, and Whittier.) Except for Whitman, Cooper, and Poe, it is difficult to think of any famous writer of the American Renaissance who is not associated with New England—even Poe was born in Boston. Towns, schools, and other institutions across the country were named after these New Englanders: for Emerson, for example, or Whittier. (Richard Nixon was born in the Quaker settlement of Whittier, California.) From this angle, one can almost say that New England is the nation; the "regions" are everywhere else.

It was a New England version of American history, for example, that penetrated the schools for the better part of the century after the Civil War. When I was in high school, in the 1950s, the U.S. history textbook my class read was written by a man named David Muzzey. I hadn't thought about that book in decades until I heard Michael Kammen mention that Muzzey came directly out of the culture of the abolitionist movement (he was born in 1870) and that his textbook was an aggressively New England–centered interpretation of U.S. history. Kammen added that even Southern high schools were obliged to use Muzzey, for lack of any "Southern" textbooks on the high school market. That is as powerful an example as I can imagine of New England's enduring cultural authority.

Let me raise one final problem. The history of old-time rural New England itself has recently come into question, and the face of the preindustrial New England village is in the process of being reevaluated. This reevaluation is largely the result of work being done by historians of material culture and geography and by archaeologists, as well as by social and cultural historians. Their findings have challenged some of our deepest assumptions. Early New England is coming to seem a newly unfamiliar place: less orderly and consensual than we used to think, more raw and "Elizabethan."[3] For example, several generations of intellectual and social historians, from Perry Miller in the 1930s to Kenneth Lockridge in the 1970s, taught us to think of early New England as following a historical trajectory that took the region from initial "Puritan" cohesiveness through a period of "declension" to a final unleashing of the individualist "Yankee" spirit. This model continues to exert considerable authority, but it has been questioned by historians who suggest that there never was a golden age of Puritan stability, that early New England may not have been so different in the first place from other New World areas settled by the British.[4]

The old contrast between Massachusetts and Virginia is no longer so clear as it used to be. Different parts of New England, even individual towns, seem to have differed from one another in their "look and feel." Indeed, the historical geographer Martyn Bowden has managed to reconstruct the English-speaking population of seventeenth-century New England in such a way as to find as many as *fourteen* distinct regions, each characterized by a different system of social, agricultural, or ideological organization.[5] The term *New England* may have been devised in the early 1600s in reference to a geographical area, but New England itself took two more centuries to become a cultural region.

The Case of Early New England Hymnody

In order to suggest something of New England's new "face," let me offer two case studies. The first is the history of early New England hymn singing, or *hymnody*. When we think of New England hymns, we probably think of generic "Protestant" religious music, four-part chorales in the tradition of Bach. But that kind of music was not sung in New England churches before the 1820s. It was introduced at that time by progressive New Englanders who were trying to "reform" what they considered the crude, uncouth, and unsophisticated music that was still being sung in the region's churches (and to polish the equally rough manner in which the music was sung).

Harriet Beecher Stowe, who can be considered the first great social historian of New England—her history took the form of a series of regional novels published after the Civil War—wrote of the "rude and primitive singing" she remembered from her childhood in Litchfield, Connecticut, in the second and third decades of the nineteenth century. One hymn she described as a "strange, wild warble, whose quaintly blended harmonies might have been learned of moaning seas or wailing winds, so strange and grand they rose, full of that intense pathos which rises over every defect of execution."[6]

This music is still performed today, and in the same energetic, nasal style, by people who live not in New England but in the South. It is the music of the Sacred Harp tradition, the practice of singing from "shape notes." That kind of singing is filled with power. There is nothing in it to suggest any befitting "New England" dignity. (Part of its power comes from the compositional convention of placing the melody line in the tenor rather than the soprano voice, a practice that allowed men and women to sing the "tune" together.) At least one modern choral group that specializes in singing this early New England music reports that they learned the appropriate vocal style only after visiting a Sacred Harp convention in Georgia.[7]

But there is more. Even those early hymns did not sound like the *earliest* New England church music. Harriet Beecher Stowe did not know that the music of her own childhood had come to New England only in the 1760s, as part of an earlier reform introduced by a group of "singing masters" who flourished between 1760 and 1820 (the most famous of those was the Bostonian William Billings). Historians of early New England church music are only now beginning to penetrate what hymnody may have sounded like back in the seventeenth and early eighteenth centuries, before the era of the singing masters. There are no published tunes to serve as guides to this earliest New England music. But one historical musicologist, Nym Cooke, has used an ingenious piece of evidence: the mocking attacks on this singing style that were published during the 1720s by a group of urbane Boston clergymen who considered it to be uncouth. Cooke has used the vivid descriptions contained in those attacks as evidence of what the music may actually have sounded like.

What Cooke has found is alien and fascinating, and it poses a challenge to any understanding I, at least, may once have had that New England Puritanism was characterized by the restraint of its piety. These early hymns were sung in unison, with the words first spoken, or "lined out," by a member of the congregation. But the music seems to have been the very opposite of dull and restrained (its closest approximation today may be found among certain Primitive Baptists from the white South). Indeed, singing in such a way could actually have been intended to generate ecstatic states of consciousness, the kinds of states that people in some other cultures have achieved by the use of drugs. Surprising, yes, but this will not be the last excursion in this essay that takes us southward in an effort to plumb the heart of New England.

The Case of the New England Town

My second case study deals with the work of historical geographers and focuses on the "New England town." The idea of a centrally arranged, or *nucleated*, New England village, with its collection of

neat white houses facing a central "common," or "green," is one
that is dear to both the American public and academic historians.
(It is one of the basic ways we have learned to distinguish early
New England from the Middle Colonies or the South.) But several
historical geographers, notably Joseph Wood and Martyn Bowden,
have recently demonstrated that such a layout was rare in early
New England. Early New England houses were not painted white,
but in bright reds, greens, or blues, as startling to look at as the
early hymns are startling to hear. More important is the physical
layout of these towns. Martyn Bowden reports that while there
were a few "compact agricultural villages" in the first few decades
of Puritan settlement, by 1650 "new settlements were dispersed
and, thereafter, most of the early compact villages experienced de-
nucleation." There was generally a patch of common land "near
the meeting of roads at the center of the New England 'town,' but
as there were few houses in this central area it certainly could not
be termed a green (encircled by houses)." Bowden concludes that
"rural New England was essentially a villageless landscape of ham-
lets and isolated farmsteads on the eve of the Revolution."

In other words, early New England even *looked* like other regions
of British North America. It was only after the American Revolution that this situation changed. According to Bowden,

> The compact New England village was born as a consequence
> of the revolution of commerce, 1790–1820. Towards the end
> of this period and extending into the 1830s many previously
> open commons acquired new institutions as well as elegant
> houses of merchants, professionals, and skilled artisans.
> Many were adorned with fences and elms. Few, if any of the
> houses were farms and none of the new villages were agricul-
> tural.[8]

By the early nineteenth century, then, after nearly two centuries
of white settlement, the "New England town" had finally come
into existence, with its central common surrounded by houses and
shops. By the 1830s these towns were invariably being described
as if that was the way they had always been. When British visitor
Charles Dickens toured New England in 1839, he was struck by
how new the towns looked:

> Every little colony of houses has its church and school-house
> peeping from among the white roofs and shady trees; every
> house is the whitest of the white; every Venetian blind the
> greenest of the green; . . . There was the usual aspect of new-
> ness on every object, of course. All the buildings looked as if
> they had been built and painted that morning, and could be
> taken down on Monday with very little trouble.[9]

Of course, Dickens never suspected that those buildings really
were new.

What matters more is the *point* of this chronology. And the point
is striking: New England town centers developed not in simple opposition to capitalism but rather as an early strategy of adapting to
it. There was little economic reason, whether in the seventeenth
century or the nineteenth, whether in New England or anywhere
else, for farmers to build their houses in the village center, miles
away from the land they tilled. But there *was* reason for shopkeep-
ers and professionals in the post-Revolutionary era to set up shop
(and home too) in just that place. The town common was central
to the entire community and also convenient to outside markets.
This was the commercializing world that Christopher Clark has recently described in his splendid book *The Roots of Rural Capitalism*.
In other words, New England came to look like "New England"
during the Federal period precisely by virtue of the presence of
shops, workshops, and small manufacturing establishments, along
with the houses of those who owned them.[10]

This explains, in turn, another startling discovery: even those
federal town centers did not look exactly the way they do today.
The commons of the early nineteenth century were not pretty-
looking "greens" surrounded by arching trees. The grass grew un-
kempt (where it grew at all) on these early commons, and much
of the land they occupied was bare or even muddy. These were
bustling places, not the serene pastoral oases reproduced on modern calendars and postcards. Their best modern counterpart would
be a cross between a shopping mall and a parking lot.

In most places, the "pastoralization" of town commons did not
take place for another generation or two, until after the Civil War.
At that time, in town after town, local Village Improvement Socie-

ties began to beautify the commons. These organizations were usually dominated by businessmen or newcomers to the community. In Amherst, Massachusetts, it was local bankers, in alliance with Amherst College, who forced the cattle and the local fairs off the town common and then reconfigured the site as a pastoral "green." In Litchfield, Connecticut, as William Butler has shown in a fascinating essay, many of these people were New Yorkers who had recently moved to town. Significantly, Litchfield was recreated as a "colonial" town only after it had lost its importance as a center of commerce, religion, and law. (In the early 1830s, Litchfield forfeited its two most important claims to regional importance: its prominent evangelical minister, Lyman Beecher, left for the greener pastures of Boston, and Tapping Reeve's famed law school closed down, the victim of competition from Yale and Harvard.) Over the next several decades new arrivals created Litchfield as a pastoral byway of Old New England, transforming Victorian buildings into "colonial" ones, planting elm trees, and making sure that neither the trolley car nor the railroad passed through the community. To "restore" their "colonial" town common, the local elite actually hired the renowned landscape architect Frederick Law Olmstead.[11]

From Section to Nation: Culture Wars

I could continue to cite such examples. But I would rather make another point: what really matters is not the sheer fact that this pastoral image of New England was actually a latter-day invention but why it became, and why it has remained, the dominant image of the region. The answer can only become clear by situating the changes I have summarized in the context of broader developments in New England's economy, social organization, and culture. To do that, it is first necessary to place the history of New England in a national context. That step is necessary because, or so I have come to suspect, a region, much like a class, is something that gets generated in the process of distinguishing itself from something else.

Let me propose such a model of conflict. Peter Onuf has shown that by the 1780s New England often acted as a self-conscious voting bloc in the U.S. Congress, working to protect its collective interests within the salient (though unofficial) sectional structure established by the Articles of Confederation. In other words, New England began to act like a separate region, or section, only when it began to interact regularly and often oppositionally with other regions. (This was also, of course, the very time when the new "New England town" was being created.) But I would suggest that New England did not fully emerge as a self-conscious cultural entity until a full generation later, during the third decade of the nineteenth century. It did so in response to two, interrelated threats to the authority of its elite groups. The first threat was posed by post-Revolutionary republican politics; the second, by the region's economic collapse during the years before and including the War of 1812.

The idealization of the New England village began in part as a cultural strategy by which members of the old local elite could maintain their social authority within a republican polity. The first prominent figure to publicize the New England village ideal was Timothy Dwight, the grandson of Jonathan Edwards, president of Yale, and a High Federalist. In his 1794 poem "Greenfield Hill," and more systematically in his posthumously published book *Travels in New England and New York*, Dwight articulated a cultural version of Federalist political theory.[12]

After 1800, New England as a region began to undergo severe economic and political decline. Jefferson's presidency undermined the national hegemony of the Federalist party: his Embargo Act of 1807, followed by the War of 1812, virtually shut down the transatlantic shipping trade, on which New England's commercial prosperity hinged. In desperation, members of the Federalist elite met at Hartford in 1814 to discuss possible defensive measures. One such measure was regional secession.[13] When the war ended in apparent glory a few months later, the Hartford Convention began to exude the unpleasant odor of a treasonable cabal. The whole debacle accelerated the disintegration of Federalism as a national force and the discrediting of the region's Federalist leadership. New England's political force seemed spent, and its economy lay in shambles. The major gainers were the Middle Atlantic and especially the South. The secretary of the Hartford Convention was Timothy Dwight's younger brother, Theodore. In the 1820s this group counterattacked, using as their weapon culture rather than politics. In 1820 the Pilgrim Society was organized by the citizens of Plymouth and Mayflower descendants elsewhere. Two years later the first full-length fictional description of the region was published, Catherine Maria Sedgwick's novel *A New-England Tale*. Catherine Sedgwick was a member of this same group: her mother was a Dwight and her father was another prominent High Federalist, Theodore Sedgwick of Stockbridge, Massachusetts, one-time Speaker of the U.S. House of Representatives. (The elder Sedgwick's efforts to suppress Shays's Rebellion in 1786 were later fictionalized in a novel by Edward Bellamy, *The Duke of Stockbridge*.) Timothy Dwight's own *Travels in New England and New York* was also published in 1822.

The cultural superiority that Dwight detected in New England—let me stay with him for a moment—had its roots precisely in the unique spatial arrangements that characterized its towns. And Dwight chose (incorrectly, as we now know) to root those arrangements in New England's colonial past. "It is a remarkable fact," he wrote, "that New England was colonized in a manner widely different from that which obtained in the other British colonies. All the ancient and a great part of the modern townships were settled in what may be called *the village manner*: the inhabitants having originally planted themselves in small towns" (Dwight's italics).

In every other part of the country, Dwight noted, people lived wherever they chose, generally on their farms, "in scattered plantations." Dwight explored at length what he saw as the historical implications of this sectional contrast. He acknowledged that living on individual scattered farms made sense in strictly economic terms, because "the farmer can more advantageously manage his own property, can oversee it more readily, and labor on it with fewer interruptions than when it is dispersed in fields at some distance from each other." But as powerful as those economic advantages might be, they were outweighed by a corresponding set of social and cultural disadvantages. Scattered farmers were reluctant to fund the construction and support of either churches or schools, or to attend them if they were constructed, since those structures would be located far from where most people actually lived. In such a way both piety and literacy, as well as refining social intercourse among different households, would suffer. As Dwight sarcastically put it, people who spend most of their time with "oxen and horses" or who talk to other families "only to make *bargains* about oxen and horses" end up much like animals themselves. "The mind, like the manners, will be distant, rough, forbidding, gross, solitary, and universally disagreeable." Dwight went on to draw the contrast between such a society and that of his own New England:

> A New Englander passing through such settlements is irresistibly struck with a wide difference between their inhabitants and those of his own country. The scene is changed at once. That intelligence and sociality, that softness and refinement which prevail even among the plain people of New England disappear, [replaced by] that repulsive character which . . . is an original feature of savage man.

Dwight drove home the larger implications of his analysis: "A nation planted in this manner can scarcely be more than half civilized." One could paraphrase Dwight's regional analysis by saying that the difference amounted to one between a *citizenry* and a *peasantry*. And the survival of America's republican political experiment was obviously in jeopardy if the nation was populated by half-civilized peasants and not socially conscious citizens. Such an educated citizenry was to be found, of course, everywhere in New England, where, as Dwight put it,

> almost the whole country is covered with villages, and every village has its church and its suite of schools. Nearly every child, even those of beggars and blacks in considerable numbers, can read, write, and keep accounts. Every child is carried to the church from the cradle, nor leaves the church but for the grave. All the people are neighbors: social beings, [they] converse, feel, sympathize, mingle minds, cherish sentiments, and are subjects of at least some degree of refinement.[14]

Here was a social description with an undisguised political agenda. And that agenda could not have been plainer: the best solution to the problem of the survival and prosperity of the rapidly expanding republic was to establish it as New England writ large.

Dwight's was only the first of a series of such accounts of New England to appear in the 1820s and 1830s. These works described and idealized the New England town as a model for the nation, as a model with which they could criticize every aspect of modern America they feared, from Jacksonian "mobocracy" and urban chaos to frontier lawlessness and, increasingly, the plantation South.[15] In order to enhance the credibility of the New England model, these writers found it useful to forget just how new it was. They described their version of New England, as we have seen, as if it went all the way back to the days of colonization. And they reappropriated the early cultural history of the region as well. For example, they discovered John Winthrop's 1630 lecture "A Model of Christian Charity," previously unpublished, and printed it for the first time in 1832. Winthrop's lecture, with its insistence on the vital need for a cooperative, regulated social life, ended with the promise that if New England succeeded, it would become a model for other, newer places, so "that men shall say of succeeding plantations, the Lord make it like that of New England."[16]

Daniel Webster, speaking at the annual Pilgrim celebration in 1850, went even further back in New England history to draw out this very point. Webster asked his audience to imagine old "Elder William Brewster" of Plymouth Colony bestowing his blessing on New England–led westward expansion:

> Spread yourselves and your children over the continent [so Brewster would surely say], accomplish the whole of your great destiny, and if it be that through the whole you carry Puritan hearts with you . . . , then will you be worthy descendants of Carver and . . . Bradford, and the rest of those who landed from stormy seas on the rock of Plymouth.

Webster went on, now in his "own" words, to predict that the United States would eventually expand beyond the boundaries of the continent and create a new *world* order in New England's image:

We have hardly begun to realize the consequences of that [1620] voyage. Heretofore the extension of our race, following our New England ancestry, has crept along the shore. But now it has extended itself. It has crossed the continent. It has not only transcended the Alleghenies, but has capped the Rocky Mountains. It is now upon the shores of the Pacific; and on this day . . . descendants of New England will there celebrate the landing. God bless them! Here's to the health and success of the California Society of Pilgrims assembled on the shores of the Pacific. And it shall yet go hard if the three hundred millions of people in China, provided they are intelligent enough to understand any thing, shall not one day hear and know something of the Rock of Plymouth too.[17]

Such rhetoric was grist for New England's mills, not only figuratively but literally too. For we should not forget that the glorification of New England's culture took place simultaneously with the region's actual industrialization. And it was industrialization, as Daniel Webster had good reason to know, that was fueling New England's economic resurgence and ensuring its ultimate cultural dominance.

For a while industrialism seemed to go hand in hand with the culture of the idealized New England village. In fact, the physical design of early factories actually resembled that of the buildings to be found on many New England town commons. Mill buildings, mill housing, even college dormitories of the 1820s and 1830s bore an uncanny (but quite natural) resemblance to one another, as anyone will see who compares the original Amherst College dormitories to the mill housing of, say, nearby Holyoke. The factory cities of Lowell and Lawrence were consciously constructed to look like "New England towns." There is another way to put that: in 1830 it was still possible to imagine that "reforming" the nation in a New England image was compatible with industrial capitalism. Both capitalism and reform could be subsumed under the larger category "progress."[18]

But of course the face of industrial capitalism soon came to contrast sharply—physically, economically, and socially—with that of the rural New England town. By the 1840s, cities like Lowell, Lawrence, and Fall River, with their ill-paid and oppressed immigrant

workers and burgeoning class conflict, were making industrial capitalism in New England indistinguishable from the "dark Satanic
mills" of old England. And it was Lowell, Lawrence, and Fall River,
not Stockbridge or Amherst or Litchfield, that were spreading New
England culture across the continent and beyond.

By then, that is, by the time of the Civil War, New England
towns themselves were being remade once again, this time in a
pastoral, "antimodern" image. It is more than an irony that the
pastoralization of the New England town was fueled by the Industrial Revolution. Even on a visual level, the mills helped the rural
towns look more "rural" by draining off first their population and
eventually their own small mills and factories, leaving a *more* rural,
less industrial townscape in their path.[19]

The people who transformed these postbellum town centers into
quaintly pastoral places believed they were simply restoring the
commons to the condition that Timothy Dwight and Catherine
Sedgwick had described a generation or two earlier. But in fact
the "traditional" look these people created, and their reasons for
creating it, differed subtly but significantly from what Dwight and
Sedgwick had known and described. The vision of New England
as small town—"our" town—ended up, willy-nilly, in the service
of industrial capitalism.

The Beechers: Battling for the West

Let me illustrate the sectional "culture wars" of the antebellum
United States—and also complicate the issue—by retelling a familiar case study, the story of a prominent man's move from New
England to the West. Rev. Lyman Beecher (1775–1863) was the
quintessential product of Federalist New England. He first achieved
prominence as an opponent of the move to "disestablish" the Congregational Church in Connecticut. But after he lost that battle,
Beecher developed a social theology that helped provide the intellectual language with which New England's Congregational establishment came to terms with emerging American democracy. In
1810 Beecher became minister to the church in Litchfield, Connecticut, where we have already encountered him. He made his
mark in Litchfield and beyond as a supporter of evangelical religion

and temperance. So effective was Beecher that in 1826 he was wooed away from Litchfield by an offer from an evangelical church in Boston. Six years later he decided to move once again, this time to accept what he considered to be an even more important post.

Beecher's new post took him to Cincinnati. There he became president of Lane Seminary, a new institution set up to train evangelical ministers in the New England mold. Cincinnati had been chosen carefully as the site of the new seminary. It lay at the very border of existing American sections, poised precisely between North and South and between East and West. Beecher's task was to prepare a cadre of evangelical ministers who would spread throughout the West and win it for the North, more precisely for New England, by forging Western communities in the image of the New England village. "If we gain the West," Beecher wrote, "all is safe; if we lose it, all is lost." [20] Indeed, if Lane should fail, and here Beecher's language mirrored that of Timothy Dwight, "our intelligence and virtue will falter and fall back into a dark minded, vicious populace—a poor, uneducated, restless mass of infuriated animalism." [21]

Beecher's agenda in Cincinnati did not include the immediate abolition of slavery. But the early 1830s were a crucial turning point in the history of American culture, a time when the kind of world Beecher believed in was about to be obliterated, not by Southerners or Jacksonian democrats, but by the radicalization of his own brand of reform. In the 1830s social reform was wrenched out of the hands of the elites who had employed it for their own purposes and taken over by new men, themselves New Englanders, men like Ralph Waldo Emerson, Charles G. Finney, and William Lloyd Garrison, the kind of individuals to whom John L. Thomas has given the enduring tag "romantic reformers." For such men, "reform" was directed at the very cultural forms that had been devised by figures like Beecher and the Dwights; that is, it was directed at the moral authority of village hierarchies. Garrison defiantly assaulted not only the institution of slavery but institutions in general, Northern as well as Southern. Emerson offered a less political but equally radical version of the same critique. As he wrote in his popular 1842 essay "Self-Reliance," "What I must do is all that concerns me, not what people think." [22]

In 1834, less than two years after Lyman Beecher moved to Cin-cinnati, Lane Seminary was all but destroyed by the new reform-ism. In that year the school was almost entirely converted to radical abolition through a series of political revival meetings led by a young Finney convert named Theodore Dwight Weld, who had been evangelized a few years earlier by Beecher's old rival Charles G. Finney. (It is somehow fitting that Weld had been named after Theodore Dwight.) Soon, Lane students—and faculty—were actu-ally engaged in political organizing among Cincinnati's African American community. The Lane trustees were appalled and, with Lyman Beecher's support, demanded a stop to this abolitionist ac-tivity. The great majority of the students and faculty resisted and finally walked out of Lane, ending up at Oberlin College, where Charles Finney himself now assumed the presidency.[23] Lane Semi-nary sputtered on for several more decades, but its momentum, and its faculty salaries, were greatly diminished.

What happened to Lane and to Beecher was what happened to "moderate" reform in general. A set of changes involving matters of ideology, generation, and class caused the center of reform to shift leftward (and in the process to be embraced by the young and the rising middle classes). New England culture would indeed prevail in the coming struggle, but it would be a somewhat differ-ently positioned New England. Lyman Beecher, for example, was opposed in 1834 by his own grown children. Among these chil-dren, of course, was Harriet Beecher Stowe; and in 1851 *she* would take up, as it were, where her father had left off some fifteen years earlier, by writing *Uncle Tom's Cabin*.

Uncle Tom's Cabin is the most stunning evangelical sermon that any Beecher ever delivered. (The loving and sacrificial deaths, first of little Eva St. Clair—her full name was "Evangeline"—then of the slave Tom, amount to two vivid retellings of the redemptive passion of Jesus on the Cross). *Uncle Tom's Cabin* is also, I would argue, the great New England regional novel. To be sure, New En-gland never actually appears—the story is set in Kentucky, Cincin-nati, New Orleans, Texas, Canada, even Africa—but *Uncle Tom's Cabin* is surely the most important book ever written about Amer-ica's great sectional conflict. In the "culture wars" of the 1850s

Harriet Beecher Stowe's novel was, as we know, a powerful weapon. It endured, and endures still, while its many imitations and parodies quickly faded. It did the evangelical work that Lane Seminary had tried and failed to accomplish.

But Harriet Beecher Stowe was not Lyman Beecher, and her critique of American culture was not exactly his. As we read *Uncle Tom's Cabin* closely from a regional perspective, something interesting starts to happen. The sections "North" and "South" seem strangely to dissolve into one another. Consider, for example, the villain of the novel, Simon Legree, the one slave owner in the book who truly is vicious. Legree surely fits (to say the least!) Timothy Dwight's description of the kind of brute one typically encounters outside New England. But Legree is as much a Yankee capitalist as he is a Southern slave owner. Stowe tells us that he was actually born in New England, in *Vermont* (one of many gratuitous touches in a book seemingly written to attack the South). Legree runs his plantation like a factory, for maximum short-term profit. He is obsessed with money, even to the point of writing financial calculations on the walls of his own parlor. In terms of regional stereotypes, he is a Yankee, not a Cavalier.

And Legree is virtually the only evil slave owner we meet. Tom's other owners, George Shelby and especially Augustine St. Clair, are very decent men trapped in an evil system, a system whose worst feature (as the novel unfolds) is that it allows Tom to lose their protection and ultimately to fall into Legree's hands. Indeed, I would like to suggest that the entire story can be plausibly, even powerfully, read as a parable of the social history of New England during the first half of the nineteenth century.

This is not the right occasion on which to draw out such a reading in any detail. But many readers, not all of them Southerners, have pointed out then and now how unrealistic Stowe's portrayal of Southern slavery is, whether she is describing the workings of a plantation or the lives and speech of the slaves themselves. Stowe had never visited the South when she wrote *Uncle Tom's Cabin*, except for a single day trip across the Ohio River into northern Kentucky. What I would suggest here is that the Kentucky farm on which we first meet Tom, the Shelby farm, resembles nothing in

Harriet Beecher Stowe's own experience so much as a Southern version of the village life she remembered as a child in Litchfield, Connecticut.

Let us look briefly at chapter 4, where we meet Tom in his neatly furnished "cabin," along with his immediate and extended family, a group that includes "young master George," the thirteen-year old son of his owner, who enters the cabin and, without ever demeaning himself, participates informally in its rich social life. Tom's wife Chloe is cooking up a feast for the neighborhood, and young master George gives Tom instruction in reading.[24] (In other contexts, Tom is described as the local "patriarch.") Life here is richly textured, "folksy," personalized, and always hierarchical. The people in the cabin—young and old, male and female, black and white—interact easily and freely with one another, with a mutual sympathy and an informality that is secured by a clear sense of their respective places in this society, places of which they are neither uncertain nor resentful.

Let me give a single example from this chapter (it is larded with similar examples). "Aunt Chloe" is able to explain to young George Shelby how one neighboring white household is beneath the Shelbys in social class. They are "'spectable folks enough in a kinder plain way" but not capable of doing anything "in style." And Chloe herself partakes proudly of the superior station of the Shelbys, in part by her very awareness of their gentility and in part by the superiority of her own *cooking* over that of the neighboring family's cook, Ginny. (Chloe cooks for the table of her master's family, and in this way she not only reflects the Shelbys' superiority but actually helps to produce it.) Ginny, Chloe points out with disdain, may be capable of "good, plain, common cooking . . . but, Lor, come to de higher branches, and what *can* she do?" Aunt Chloe sums up a whole cultural universe when she admonishes her owner's young son with a sigh: "Ah, Mas'r George, you doesn't know half your privileges in yer family and bringin' up!"

That cultural universe is essentially Stowe's own. Let me reiterate something that may not be easy for Americans living in the late twentieth century to fathom: there is no irony here (except of the gentlest sort), no criticism of Aunt Chloe's perspective, no subtle condemnation of the implicit racism (or the explicit acceptance of class differences) in this folksy picture. The associations that Stowe is trying to evoke here are all positive; life on the Shelby farm, even in "Uncle Tom's cabin," is close to idyllic. There is only a single flaw in the idyll: what makes chapter 4 so poignant to read is that the reader already knows that Tom's pleasant days are doomed to end, for he is about to be sold. But take away the buying and selling, the penetration of market relations, and this is a portrait of the kind of community that Timothy Dwight might have found strangely familiar, *almost like home.*

Remember that Stowe would devote the rest of her long literary career to writing local-color novels about life in old New England. In fact, the rural dialect in those novels is strikingly similar to the "black" dialect we encounter in *Uncle Tom's Cabin.* From that angle, the fourth chapter of that great novel can be said to constitute Stowe's first New England local-color portrait.

At the other end of the novel is the Legree plantation, where Tom for the first time encounters suffering. If the Shelby farm points back to the New England that Harriet Beecher Stowe remembered from her youth, the Legree plantation points to the New England to which she had returned shortly before she began to write *Uncle Tom's Cabin.* From that same angle, then, one can read Uncle Tom's tragic journey "down the river" from his old Kentucky home to Legree's hellish plantation on the Red River as a *spatial* representation of Stowe's own journey through *time,* from early-nineteenth-century small-town New England to the mid-nineteenth-century industrial landscape.

Indeed, one of the things that makes *Uncle Tom's Cabin* so powerful as a political *and* a literary document is the way it explicitly blurs the easy distinction between North and South, between slavery and industrial capitalism. *Uncle Tom's Cabin* achieves its greatest force in its critique not just of slavery alone but of the heartless exploitation of labor that was coming to underlie modern Western society as a whole. At one point Augustine St. Clair says: "Look at the high and the low, all the world over, and it's the same story,— the lower class used up, body, soul, and spirit, for the good of the upper." Or again, that the slave owner "is only doing, in another form, what . . . capitalists are doing by the lower classes; that is . . . appropriating them . . . to their use and convenience. . . . [The laborer] is as much at the will of his employer as if he were sold to him. The slave owner can whip his slave to death,—the capitalist can starve him to death." St. Clair even predicts a coming revolution: "I tell you, if there is anything that is revealed with the strength of a divine law in our time, it is that the masses are to rise, and the under class become the upper one."[25]

Stowe is no Marxist, though. Rather, her critique is that of an antebellum New England patrician, an evangelical version of the perspective she inherited from her older New England colleagues Timothy Dwight and Catherine Sedgwick. What Stowe had glimpsed—and faced, for the one and only time—was that New England had betrayed its identity, that it had become one of the very societies that her father's generation had warned would emerge if the rest of the country failed to reform in the image of the New England village. It was Lyman Beecher himself who had warned that in such a case the nation would be populated by a "dark minded, vicious . . . uneducated, restless mass of infuriated animalism." That was what had indeed happened, not just in the West or the South, but in America's moral heartland, New England itself. If moral progress and industrial capitalism seemed comfortably wedded together in 1830, then by 1850—at the moment of *Uncle Tom's Cabin*—it had become clear to some few, Harriet Beecher Stowe among them, that the marriage had come apart.

From Section to Region

As industrial New England won the national culture wars, so New England as a "region" was left the old image of village life, New England as "Our Town." That image was often promulgated by the very people who had made their money, directly or indirectly, from the Industrial Revolution. As we have seen, the New England town was pastoralized in the postbellum period, a consequence of the "antimodernist" sensibility that also produced the "colonial revival," as a retreat from the world these people (or their parents) had helped to make.

In literature this was the period of regional "local color" writing. Sarah Orne Jewett, Mary Wilkins, even Robert E. Frost, were regional writers more than national ones (just as the earlier New

England writers—Hawthorne, Emerson, and the rest—were by now national writers). And it is no accident that most of these New England local colorists wrote about *northern* New England—New Hampshire, Vermont, Maine. One of Frost's early books of poetry was carefully titled *North of Boston*. (Frost was born in 1868, not in New England, but in San Francisco, where his father, a Copperhead Democrat, had gone at the time of the Civil War. Robert Frost's name was actually *Robert E. Lee Frost*.)

It was Harriet Beecher Stowe who became the first New England regional writer, retreating after the Civil War from the heavy social criticism of *Uncle Tom's Cabin* into the elegant local history of *The Minister's Wooing, Oldtown Folks, Poganuc People*, and other novels, books that came, each one more than the last, to sentimentalize New England's village past. Or take John Greenleaf Whittier, a writer who likewise first won fame in the antebellum years as the highly politicized poet of abolition, but who became even better known after the War as the author of "Snowbound," an elegiac evocation of region and childhood (and, given the fact that it was published as early as 1866, a poem that was apolitical almost to the point of amnesia). Much like Stowe, Whittier first achieved renown as a "sectional" writer; also like her, he became accepted as a "national" writer by turning to regional local color. It is significant that the literature of local color was written not for regional audiences but for a national one.[26] The regionalist movement, one might say, assumed and depended upon the existence of a cultural center. In this way aggressive antebellum sectionalism became transmuted into nostalgic postbellum regionalism.

Remember too that the "sectional" New England literature of the pre-1850 period was not about the region's past but about its present. Writers like Timothy Dwight and Catherine Sedgwick surely *idealized* their subject, but (there is an important difference here) they did not *sentimentalize* it. The pastoral New England town created in the postbellum years both in literature and in landscape was a far cry from the dynamic, protocapitalist New England villages of the Federal era.

The pastoralization of New England continues to this day, abetted by calendars, tourists, and the ebbing of the Industrial Revolution. Just recently I heard the publisher of *Yankee* magazine assert with considerable pride (mixed, I can only hope, with a little irony) that "New England looks more like New England now than it did thirty years ago." The publisher's pride in that statement came from his knowledge that *Yankee* magazine itself had played no small role in New England's ongoing invention.

Coda: The New England That Wasn't

Twice in this essay—the first time with music, the second with literature—we have traveled south and west in order to discover the soul of New England. Our final trip will be in the opposite direction, to New England's northeast. I am referring to Canada's Maritime Provinces, New Brunswick, Nova Scotia, and Prince Edward Island. I visited the Maritimes in 1993 under the sponsorship of the United States Information Agency (USIA), consulting there with university faculty who specialized in what they accurately term "United States Studies." But in the course of my visit I learned more about my own New England than about Canada itself.

There are obvious similarities between New England and the Maritime Provinces. The two regions are contiguous. More than that, they are similar in topography, constituting in effect a single bioregion (surely Maine "ought" to be one of the Maritimes). Indeed, New England and the Maritimes are lumped together as a single region in Joel Garreau's engaging 1981 book *The Nine Nations of North America*.[27] And their respective histories, too, have been long and deeply interlinked.

But the contrast between the two regions was what surprised me. I had gone to Canada expecting the Maritime Provinces to be, as the New England states are, at the very center of their national culture. What I found was that the Maritimes are actually close to the *margins* of Canadian culture. They have no Boston to rival (or surpass) Toronto's New York. *Eastern Canada*, I learned, refers not to the Maritimes but to Ontario, two full provinces to the west.

Nothing brought out this cultural contrast more clearly than the fact that several years earlier, as I learned, I had been preceded to Canada, on a similar mission for the USIA, by my friend Robert A. Gross, director of the American Studies program at the College of William and Mary. Gross had visited every region of Canada *except*

the Maritime Provinces. On my own visit to the Maritimes nobody
I spoke to was surprised that their region had been left out of Bob
Gross's itinerary; indeed, only a few of them were even aware that
he had been to Canada at all. Just try to imagine a visiting academic from, say, China, undertaking a comprehensive tour of uni-
versities in the United States without including New England on
his or her assigned route!

Why such a difference? Why is it that New England is at the
center of its national culture, while the Maritime Provinces are at
the margins of theirs? The reasons are of course complex, but
surely they have something to do with the economic and political
histories of the two regions. Let me suggest here only the most
obvious point. As early centers of transatlantic and coastal shipping, both New England and the Maritime Provinces achieved
commercial prosperity by the early nineteenth century. But commercial prosperity did not endure in either region, as north-south
shipping routes came to be replaced by east-west rail routes and
wooden ships were replaced by metal ones. In nineteenth-century
New England, as we know, commercial capital was reinvested on
a large scale in industrial manufacturing and later in Western extractive industry—the story I have just been retelling. But such a
change was exactly what did *not* take place in the Maritimes.
There, wealthy merchants invested in other kinds of ventures, ventures that did not pay off nearly so well as New England's did.[28] A
vicious cycle ensued, and by the twentieth century the Maritime
elite lacked the influence that would have enabled them to get railroad routes to link them with Toronto and other commercial centers. The Maritime Provinces, you might say, *lost* their Civil War.
And they continue today to live with the consequences of that defeat. Their political force is spent, and their economy lies in shambles. Neither their landscape nor their history has been pastoralized. Today the people of that ever so New England–like region
remind me, in their sense of almost cosmic fatalism, defeat, and
loss, of nothing so much as, yes, the postbellum American South.

3 • What We Talk about When We Talk about the South

Edward L. Ayers

Given all that has been written and said about the South, we might expect that Americans would be able to think clearly about the region. Yet television, movies, novels, roadside markers, old history books, and jokes tell the same basic stories about the South over and over, even when people know they are not true to their own experience or to the complexity of human life. When Southerners meet people from other places they know that those non-Southerners know the stories too—and believe some of them. One Virginian who went to Harvard in the early 1980s fantasized about putting a sign around his neck to foreclose some of the questions he repeatedly faced, or imagined he faced: "Yes, I am from the South. No, I do not know your uncle in Mobile. No, I was not born there. Both of my parents, in fact, are literate. No, I do not like Molly Hatchet. No, I do not watch 'Hee Haw.' No, I do not own slaves. No, I do not want any. Thank you very much. Have a nice day." He concluded that the sign strategy would not work, though, "because everyone would think someone else had written it for me, probably so I wouldn't have to memorize it."[1]

Geographers have noted that Americans, with remarkable uniformity and consistency, picture their country's regions in ways that blur their diverse human characteristics into stereotypes. One of the chief features of that imagined map is the Southern Trough, which cuts across Mississippi and Alabama, embracing parts of Arkansas, Louisiana, and Georgia at the edges. This trough appears to most Americans as the least desirable place in the United States to live. Other Southern states cannot take too much grim comfort from such disparagement of their Deep South neighbors, for the sides of the trough rise only gradually until they reach the usual boundaries of what Americans take to be the North, the Midwest, and the West. The whole South appears to be a vast saucer of unpleasant associations.[2]

Polls tell us, however, that white Southerners are the Americans most satisfied with their home states. In their eyes, the Southern Trough is a sheltered valley, shielded from the most corrosive effects of Yankee greed and rudeness. These white Southerners believe they live in the best part of the United States. People from elsewhere in the country look down on Southerners, they believe, only because these other Americans do not really know the South and its residents.[3]

Things are especially complicated for black Southerners. "It seems very often that blacks in the North feel themselves superior to blacks in the South," Eddy Harris, a non-Southern black man, reported recently, "because they think blacks in the South were simple-minded enough to stay and suffer the worst of the horrors and indignities. Southern blacks too often are called 'Bamas' and country niggers, and are seen as backward and uneducated." But Southern blacks are just as confident as their white neighbors that non-Southerners just don't get it. As an African American Southerner told Harris, "Blacks in the South look down on blacks in the North. 'They're up there killing each other, doing the white man's work,' he said. 'They escaped to the Promised Land and got handed a bunch of lies. Now they don't know what to do.' " The South, by contrast, appears at least knowable, predictable. Many Northern blacks see in the South the foundation for their own virtues, and they see a return to those virtues as the best hope of beleaguered Northern communities.[4]

Perhaps reflecting such views, the tide of black migration has turned. For decades after slavery black Southerners escaped the South at the first opportunity; now many more blacks are moving to the South than are leaving. The top five destinations for migrating black Americans at the end of the twentieth century are all

Southern cities. Eddy Harris, after traveling throughout the South, came to wonder if he had not been wrong about the region: "I tried to remember why I had come to the South in the first place, what I had expected to find. White people shooting at me. Black people bitching and moaning. A reason to hate this place. Or was I looking for a reason to love this place? I really didn't know anymore." Harris found himself asking the question many black Americans have apparently asked themselves: What "irrational love" of the South "have I inherited, do I harbor and long to admit? In what weird ways is the South not just an ancestral home, but my home as well? How much of this place is within me?" [5]

Some African Americans have found, to their surprise, that the South exerts the emotional pull of a homeland, more palpable and credible than an Africa whose landscape and language they do not know. The South has always had a different moral geography for blacks and whites; its history has always had a different trajectory. Black Southerners have not loved "The South" as it has been symbolized so frequently: no flags, monuments, or anthems have connected black Southerners with the official South. But black Americans have made parts of Southern states their own through sweat and sacrifice; they have loved certain farms, houses, and streets. The South for these Southerners is—as it was for William Faulkner and Thomas Wolfe—a place to love and a place to hate, a place impossible to figure out. [6]

As defenders of the South claim, it is not easily understood by outsiders; as its critics claim, it is apparently not understood much better by its resident defenders. The South has suffered from generalizations that trivialize it, whether those generalizations take the form of romantic and nostalgic dreams of the past, arrogant regional stereotypes, or scholarly arguments about central themes and unifying characteristics. Positive or negative, these images of the South keep us from seeing the people of the region with the fullness and empathy all people deserve.

Polls show us that Americans from all over the country picture the South as backward-looking. From the positive point of view, Southerners seem to respect the past, the land, and their elders. From the negative point of view, the South appears to be dominated by nostalgia and dullness. These images are different sides of the same coin, different aspects of the basic story we tell ourselves about the South: it is the American place where modern life has not fully arrived, for good and for ill.

People have not merely made up this story from whole cloth. There can be no doubt that the South has been poorer than the rest of the country, less technologically advanced, more wedded to racial exploitation and segregation. But when the South is portrayed as a "culture" or "society," even a "civilization," that stands as the binary opposite of the North, a relative situation tends to become an absolute characteristic; Southern differences with the North are transformed into traits that mark the very soul of the Southern people. Even the most original historian of the relationship between the South and the nation argued that students of the region "should not be concerned indiscriminately with everything that occurs within the South," but should focus only at those "points where the conditions of the Southern region differ from those of other regions." This assumption underlies much of Southern studies. Without obvious and clearly demarcated difference, it appears, there is no justification for Southern history.[7]

People realize that when they speak of "Southern culture" they are creating a fiction, a fiction of a geographically bounded and coherent set of attributes to be set off against a mythical non-South. Accordingly, people try to introduce complexity by qualifying the idea of the South, pointing out that the mountains are different from the lowlands, that whites are different from blacks, men from women, rich from poor. Often, those who speak with the greatest conviction about the reality of a Southern culture are those who most emphasize its internal diversity. Yet the very language of "Southern culture" suggests that there are hidden ligaments and tissues holding it all together in some way.

Anthropologists, from whom historians over the years have borrowed their notions of cultures as systems, things, templates, and possessions, have recently warned us to quit thinking in these metaphors. As soon as we speak of cultures, they point out, we begin to "essentialize," as the jargon has it, to locate in some other people an essence of what they really are; to "exoticize," to focus on and exaggerate the difference between one's self and the object of contemplation; to "totalize," to make "specific features of a society's thought or practice not only its essence but also its totality." We draw boundaries between things we call cultures and then fill in those boundaries with something to make the boundaries meaningful.[8]

Americans believe, hope the South is different and so tend to look for differences to confirm that belief, that "knowledge." White Southerners are, until proven otherwise, traditional, backward, obsessed with the past, friendly, potentially violent, racist, and polite. Black Southerners are, until evidence is presented to the contrary, more friendly and down-home than their Northern counterparts, more conservative and religious. When Southerners do not behave in these ways, they are deemed less Southern, less fitted to the place where they live, exceptions. Some see such people as more cosmopolitan, others as Yankee wanna-bes, ashamed of what should be their real identity.

The South plays a key role in the nation's self-image: the role of evil tendencies overcome, mistakes atoned for, progress yet to be made. Before it can play that role effectively, the South has to be set apart as a distinct place that has certain fundamental characteristics. As a result, Southern difference is continually being recreated and reinforced. Americans, black and white, somehow need to know that the South is different and so tend to look for differences to confirm that belief. This is not something that is only done *to* the South by malevolent, insensitive non-Southerners. The North and the South have conspired to create each other's identity as well as their own. The South eagerly defines itself against the North, advertising itself as more earthy, more devoted to family values, more spiritual, and then is furious to have things turned around, to hear itself called hick, phony, and superstitious. The South feeds the sense of difference and then resents the consequences.

Southerners with something to sell traffic in difference, eagerly marketing any distinctiveness they can claim, especially now that the Southern black freedom movement and the spread of racial conflict in the North and West have made the South seem less uniquely repugnant. Culture is a great natural resource: it is as renewable as trees, as deep as mines. Each state has found its unique vein: Virginia quarries its Jeffersonian period, while Georgia sells burning Atlanta, Mississippi and Alabama fight over who is the deeper South, Tennessee offers country music, Kentucky tenders bluegrass, and Louisiana hawks Cajun. North Carolina even has a vaguely Orwellian-sounding branch of government called the Department of Cultural Resources. There is, accordingly, an unmistakable tendency for so-called cultural traits to coincide with state boundaries. Notice the architecture of the welcome stations along the interstates, with white columns at the portals of South Carolina and Mississippi, eighteenth-century plantation houses when you enter Virginia, and log cabin themes when you roll into Tennessee a few hundred yards away. Think of the names of state university athletic mascots: Cavaliers, Rebels, Volunteers—all rich with (white) historical connotation, all accentuating the differences at the state lines.[9]

The South needs these internal differences. With tourism as one of its major industries, the South, like other places, needs as much diversity as it can be made to contain, as many subregional cookbooks as it can produce, as many license plates and commemorative T-shirts, as many institutes, journals, encyclopedias, and historians. A considerable portion of what we see as Southern culture is manufactured to order. People want to manage, enhance, manufacture memory, to be a part of something larger than themselves. Throughout the modern era traditions have been invented on the spot—the kilt, for example, or Betsy Ross—giving a satisfying pedigree to something that is in fact much newer or more ad hoc. The idea of the "Old" South was in some ways a sales job in the first place, given that at the time of the Civil War many of the plantation districts of Mississippi, Texas, and Arkansas were no older than many of today's subdivisions. Now, in turn, new places often try to distill an essence of the imagined old ones: shopping centers wear the regalia of plantations, and housing developments dress as old villages. Even chain restaurants, the very symbol of standardization, cater to the longing for folksiness. Enormous and efficient establishments called "The Cracker Barrel," set up for business along the interstates, are bedecked with rocking chairs, rough stone fireplaces, and the merchandise of country stores.[10]

I once visited my grandparents in their small town in the mountains of western North Carolina on a Saturday. That day the town square was filled with a mountain craft fair. People lined up to try the apple butter simmering in the iron kettle, to watch the dolls dance on the board, to admire the quilters' work, to listen to the fiddle music. I had no time to dawdle, since my grandparents were waiting for me, so I stopped in for a fast burger at the new Hardee's on the bypass. Being Southern, I automatically made conversation with the young woman behind the counter as she filled my order. "Nice craft fair," I imaginatively offered. "Yeah, I guess," she said in her mountain accent as she poured the sweetened iced tea into the cup emblazoned with the corporate logo. "Have you ever seen so many Yankees in your life?" And sure enough, I noticed when I dropped in later, the cars parked all around the square were from Pennsylvania, Florida, or New York. In fact, upon examination, it appeared that many of the authentic artisans were also Yankees, or at least yuppies. The crafts may have been of authentic Appalachian style, celebrating the mountain heritage (the name of the county's high school), but the people in the overalls and gingham were not. Using what we imagine to be "authenticity" as a unit of measurement unfairly devalues both the young woman in the Hardee's and the people practicing crafts.

It seems only commonsensical that an older culture that has somehow managed to persist into the present would be on the verge of fading away. The bucket of Southern distinctiveness, it appears, was full up to the brim in 1865 but has been leaking faster and faster ever since. The experience of those who now live in the South, with its confusion, complications, and compromises, seems less fully Southern than the society that came before, which appears to have been more unified and coherent. The lovingly recreated models of log cabins, plantation homes, forts, and villages that dot the South try to recapture the authentic history, untainted by time, change, or contact with the outside world. Today's experiences of Wal-Mart, country radio, and NASCAR, by contrast, seem somehow less organically related to the region, the products of infection by mass communication and business.

Ironically, though, Southerners have always held similar fears. For as long as people have believed there was a South they have also believed it was disappearing. Virginians and Carolinians thought the South was dying as early as the 1830s, when too much easy money in the Cotton Kingdom pulled people to raw places such as Alabama and Mississippi, which knew nothing of true Southern gentility. Then people felt certain that the South would be erased by the end of slavery or Reconstruction. They did not expect the South to survive the effects of automobiles or radios, of World War II and the postwar bulldozer revolution. There was reason to believe that the events of Brown v. Board of Education, Montgomery, Greensboro, Selma, and Birmingham might kill off the South. If that did not do the trick, surely the inexorable spread of strip malls, fast-food places, cable, and satellite dishes marked the end of the South.[11]

From its very beginning, people have believed that the South, defined against an earlier South that was somehow more authentic, more real, more unified and distinct, was not only disappearing but also declining. Jefferson's South declined into the delusion of Calhoun's South, which declined into the incompetency of Jefferson Davis's South, which declined into the corruption of the carpetbaggers' South, which declined into the poverty and inbreeding of Faulkner's South, which declined into the race baiting of George Wallace's South, which declined into the scandals of Jim Bakker and Jimmy Swaggart. The South has always seemed to live on the edge of extinction, the good as well as the bad perpetually disappearing. The writer John Egerton recently begged his fellow Southerners to realize that "all our strengths—of family and history and tradition, of geography and climate, of music and food, of spoken and written language—are endangered treasures."[12]

But the South, perpetually fading, seems also to be perpetually with us. Sociologists have measured the shape and depth of Southern distinctiveness and found that the perception of it does not disappear as we might expect, that education and contact with the non-South actually heighten Southern self-consciousness. In much the same way that "Italians" or "Germans" were imbued with a common identity only when they arrived in the United States, white "Southerners" have often found commonalities generated by mass media or outsiders. Lowlanders and highlanders, old families and new, residents of Charleston, South Carolina, and of Charleston, West Virginia, Episcopalians and Southern Baptists, all find that they are "Southerners," kin, away from home.

People apparently need to be able to think in spatial terms, to identify various facets of "national character" with various places within the nation, to find people who embody some set of traits that others find especially attractive or, more often, repellent or problematic. Americans, of course, are not alone in this need: throughout the world, people tend to divide national character along various lines, often along a North-South axis. In one society after another, Northerners see themselves as economically vigorous, industrious, hardworking, reliable, serious, and thrifty, while Southerners see themselves as socially refined, patient, obliging, amiable, and generous.[13]

Stories about the South tend to be stories about what it means to be modern. The South often appears as the locus of the nonmodern (as in so much country music or in *Mayberry, R.F.D* or *The Waltons*), or of the modern world gone bad (as in *Deliverance* or *Cape Fear* or Walker Percy's novels). People have long projected onto the South their longing for a place free from the pressures of making a profit, free from loneliness and isolation; for just as long, others have projected onto the South the disgust, and maybe anxiety, they feel toward those who are unable or unwilling to keep up with the headlong rush into the future. The South is made to bear a lot of metaphorical baggage.[14]

The South has become an object of fun, a sanctioned way to laugh at poverty and backwardness in a way that has been banished for every other group. Pathetically enough, Southerners seem to have a habit of projecting ridicule onto the Southern state next to them, especially if it happens to be a bit poorer. For example: Why can't they take a group photo of the people in ———— (insert the name of your favorite object of ridicule here)? Because every time the photographer yells "Cheese," all the people line up single file for a government handout. Or: What is the state flower of ———— (insert the name of your least favorite Southern state here)? The satellite dish. Inbreeding seems to be an especially popular topic for these jokes, signifying the South's isolation and perversion born of being out of the mainstream of American life.

Why is it that these jokes are culturally sanctioned, that it is deemed permissible to make jokes about white Southerners that we can make about no one else? I think it is partly because white Southerners are not "really" ethnic; they are not marked by certain physical features, certain kinds of family names, or a certain religion, the markers we recognize as authentic, as so powerful as to be above humor. It is also because white Southerners, with their slavery, their racism, and their attachment to the past, seem to have brought on their own troubles. And it is because Southerners, ambivalent about their place in the nation, tell the jokes about their fellow Southerners as a way of inoculating themselves against the same jokes being told against them. Like a member of a "true" ethnic group, a white Southerner is expected to be conscious of his or her regional identity—not fanatical but not indifferent. To be fanatical is to be sadly wedded to a lost cause; to ignore it is to pretend to be something one is not. The line between the two is a fine one.[15]

Accent is the closest attribute white Southerners have to a physical marker to separate them from other white Americans; the same is true among blacks. These accents, which may seem a trivial, vestigial, difference are in fact rich in meaning and consequence. Precisely because language, unlike physical attributes, seems to be at least partly under the control of its speaker, it is often taken as the key measure of national belonging. Accent accentuates difference where there is supposed to be commonality; it testifies to an inability or unwillingness to go along, to fit in. In the American case, accent is a marker of class and economic integration as well as regional identity. A Southern accent is often understood, inside the South as well as beyond its borders, as a symbol of poor education, low ambition, and reactionary politics.

Southern accents, in fact, offer a useful way to understand the evolution of the South. Despite the imagined organic connections between culture and environment, for example, according to which it is assumed that Southerners, because of their hot and debilitating climate, speak more slowly than people from other places, they do not. In fact, they speak about the same number words in a given time as other Americans; those in the hottest parts of the South do not talk more slowly than their upcountry counterparts. The widespread notions that people in isolated pockets of the region, such as mountains or islands, speak some vestige of "pure" Elizabethan English are, as one linguist puts it, "pretty much complete exaggerations." Southern accents were first commented on only in the mid-nineteenth century; a Southern accent may not have developed until whites and blacks assimilated with one another over a broad enough area to forge a common way of speaking.[16]

While vocabulary in the South is converging with that in the rest of the country, grammar and pronunciation do not seem to be. Young people, especially women, drawl as much as older ones. In fact, Southern speech is becoming more distinct in some ways: the younger a person is, regardless of education, the more likely he or she is to pronounce *hem* like *him* and *pen* like *pin*. It appears, finally, that migrants from the North are more likely to adapt to Southern speech patterns than to set an example for their new neighbors to emulate. In all these ways, the image of a naturally adapted, artifactual, and disappearing South seems belied by careful study of current practices.

The almost habitual identification of Southern culture with certain traits tends quickly to stereotype, as certain subregions, subgeographies, classes, genders, or races become identified as carriers of certain characteristics. These traits, in turn, are given varying moral meanings, depending on the use to which they are put. Most of the debates over Southern culture over the generations have involved, for the most part, switching the moral value attached to a given trait. Thus plain folk, who were long seen as without ambition, are now seen as demonstrating a healthy aversion to the soulless capitalist market; former slaves, whom previous generations of Northern and Southern whites saw as lazy, were actually exercising their independence against white employers; planters that many people in the nation thought were gracious and paternalistic were actually pretentious and patronizing. Many of the imagined traits, in other words, have remained the same; we merely change their meaning to suit our purposes.

We tend to tell the story of this distinct South from the relatively narrow point of view of our nation-state; we are provincial in our understanding of provinciality. The traditional, poor, and leisurely South takes on a different aspect when we step offshore, when we take a perspective not defined by the bounds of the nation-state. From the viewpoint of the Caribbean or much of South America, or even parts of Europe, the American South appears to have been rich and money-driven throughout its history. From the perspective of nineteenth-century Brazil, for example, the other great slave society of the hemisphere, the nineteenth-century South was a land of cities and towns, railroads and steamboats, white democracy and equality. From the perspective of people of African descent elsewhere in the world, the South appeared not only as a place of lynching and segregation but also as a place of relative black progress and possibility. Rather than the exception, the South becomes mostly American.[17]

But Americans seldom portray the South that way. Instead, it appears as the tropical corner of the nation, as the Latin America of North America. We rarely see movies or television shows set in the cold winters of Alabama or Texas, the ice storms of Georgia and Tennessee. Cotton bolls are always bursting white, heat rises in waves off the blacktop in a place where it seems always to be August. In fact, many people see geography as the reason why the South inevitably took the shape that it did, why the Civil War tore the nation in two along a natural, almost perforated line. Despite generations of historians' work, many Americans still believe that the Civil War was the unavoidable result of an agrarian economy locked in battle with its natural adversary to the North, a sort of blameless struggle between the old and the new. The war seemed to await only the development of the North into an industrial economy sufficiently modern to resent and overpower its rural adversary. After passing through something like an adolescent crisis, the nation could get on with its destiny.

But did the North and South simply ripen into what they were destined to be all along? Few would have thought so in 1800, nearly two hundred years after English and Africans began to arrive. It was only then, as the Industrial Revolution in Britain geared up, that the South became The Cotton South. The Southern landscape has proven itself remarkably adaptable ever since, the "natural" landscape for backwoods farmers, opulent planters, coal miners, discount-store magnates, soybean farmers, and toxic-waste dumpers. The South trails off into the North and the West in a disappointingly vague way, as it did in 1861 until bloody guerrilla conflicts and presidential strong-arming decided where the region ended for the time.[18]

In fact, there was never a time when Southern culture developed secure from the outside, when people knew just where the borders were, when people knew just what the South was and was not. From the eighteenth century to the present, Southerners of every sort have lived at the intersection of many lines of influence. Power and prestige often have come not merely as the result of knowing the right people locally, of marrying into the right neighborhood family. It was the white man who knew what was going on in the state capital and in Washington that had the most power, the man who had access to capital and information from New York or London that really made money. The political power and credit, in turn, allowed a man to hold office, to build a mansion, to become, ironically, most stereotypically "Southern." Perhaps most tellingly, it was the men who went to West Point, who served the United States in its war with Mexico, that became identified as the prototypical white Southerners: Jefferson Davis and Robert E. Lee.[19]

From its very beginning, the white South saw itself as a particular strain of British culture, adapting parts of British identity that seemed to fit at the time. In the earliest days of the Chesapeake, military models provided the standard; as men and women began to establish farms to grow tobacco, the English yeomanry provided the script; as the farms grew into larger plantations worked by slaves, younger sons of the English gentry created an image of themselves as landed aristocrats. There was nothing dishonest or delusional about this; these white Southerners thought of themselves as colonial Englishmen. Just as other Englishmen abroad later wore pith helmets and operated mines, Southern Englishmen owned slaves and ran plantations. Southerners, in fact, did not so much emulate the North as borrow many of the same materials from England that the North borrowed. Sometimes, as with the cult of honor, the North borrowed something only to jettison it in a few decades, while the South held on for generations longer.

The black people of the South made their own adjustments, holding on to what they could of Africa, taking what they were forced to take or what they wanted to take of Britain. As generations passed, a distinctly African American set of practices and styles developed and spread across the face of the South. Neither white nor black Southerners, of course, failed to see the differences between themselves and those of other skin color. African American Southerners reveled in their music, their crafts, their language, and their collective memories; European Southerners reveled in their literacy, their technology, and their political power. Yet many commonalities between black and white emerged, with influences running in both directions, sometimes in obvious ways, sometimes almost imperceptibly. White and black, despite their hatred and mutual suspicion, found that their taste in food, in speech, and in religion came to bear strong affinities.

Evangelicalism exemplifies the way nineteenth-century Southern culture developed. Evangelical religion became, over several decades, the great continuity and commonality in Southern culture. But it was not there at all at the beginning, when Englishmen from certain parts of the homeland supposedly brought the germ of Southern culture with them. Rather, heart religion was imported from England and took on a peculiarly Southern style because of the contribution of, and the problems presented by, African Americans. The importation of Baptists and Methodists came a full 150 years after Jamestown, but now it is religion that seems to set the South apart the most: it is religion that is the basis for much of its political conservatism, that earns it the name Bible Belt, that seems to grow stronger.

The South's most distinctive political feature, its stark biracialism, also constantly reflected changes in the larger Atlantic world. The preferred mode of white dominion changed from that of a distant patriarch in the eighteenth century to a "softer" kind of paternalism in the Victorian era to a kind of managerial race relations in the late nineteenth and early twentieth centuries. In every instance, white Southerners followed the best ideals of European, especially English, dominion. They were not merely trying to please the metropole, but were doing what they did in other facets of their lives: trying to make the best deal they could with the central ideas and tenets of the civilization of which they considered themselves a part while maintaining their divergent economic interests and their pride.

It was for this reason that white Southerners felt so wounded and outraged when they were charged with inhumanity as slaveholders. They claimed, with some justice, that they were doing

nothing that Northerners and Englishmen had not done for generations, nothing that the Bible and the Constitution did not at least
tacitly sanction. The rules seemed to change virtually overnight.
The white South charged that it was the North that was changing,
that was altering the script. White Southerners, finding themselves
on the defensive, quickly began to do something they had not done
before, namely, to assemble, entirely from materials available in
the larger Anglo-American culture, a picture of themselves as a
distinctive people with a separate history, culture, and destiny.

During the high tide of antebellum culture and sectionalism, in
the 1850s, white Southern nationalists eagerly pored over the
newspapers, journals, and books of Britain and Europe, finding
there raw material with which to create a vision of the South as a
misunderstood place. Sir Walter Scott, Lord Byron, Goethe, Italian
and German nationalists, Karl Marx—they all helped create an image of people in search of their true identities, in conflict with the
materialistic modern world. White Southern slaveholders did not
merely find themselves different, naturally and organically, and
then rebel as a result; rather, they created an idiom of exaggerated,
coherent uniqueness out of European ideals because they felt that
their erstwhile countrymen had rebelled against them. Slavery provided the impetus, but Britain, Europe, and the North supplied the
language, the audience Southerners sought to appease, and the
people against whom they defined themselves. The commonality
as well as the difference fed the Civil War.[20]

The founders of the Confederacy saw themselves as participating
in a widespread European movement, toward the self-deter-
mination of a people to be contained within its "natural" boundaries, boundaries that coincided with economic interests, with
shared beliefs, with a way of life. As the Confederacy was born,
people throughout the South recognized the need for all the para-
phernalia of a nation and made it up on the spot. They used such
modern means as contests advertised in newspapers and facsimiles
of the founding Confederate documents suitable for framing.
Southerners had paid close attention throughout the 1840s and
1850s to the strategies of European nationalists and were ready,
even if, as Drew Faust has put it, "the emphasis placed by European nationalist thinkers on political differentiation based on sepa-

rate race, language, religion, and history was problematic for white, English-speaking southerners." Like other nationalists in other places then and since, forced to make the most of trivial, even nonexistent, cultural differences, white Southerners invested their nation with what they imagined to be a "racial" difference between the cold Anglo-Saxons of the North and their own heated Norman heritage. Confederates exhorted their countrymen to purge their language of Yankeeisms or Africanisms, to speak no "corrupt provincial dialect, but the noble undefiled English language." The Confederacy did not think of itself as something new, a dangerous experiment, but as the natural embodiment of something well established.[21]

The Confederacy was hardly unique in the self-conscious way it came into being. Nations have been built of less sturdy economic and cultural materials. In fact, we are now beginning to see that, as a recent study of nationalism has put it, "most nations have always been culturally and ethnically diverse, problematic, protean and artificial constructs that take shape very quickly and come apart just as fast." Even England, the first modern nation, found a common identity only in opposition to France. The problem of the Confederacy was that its defining war came before the Southern nation was much more than an idea, before any deep or wide identity of its people as Southerners—rather than as Virginians, Carolinians, or Texans, say—could develop.[22]

The entire Civil War was an extraordinarily unlikely event. While people long predicted some sort of conflict, few people, North or South, would have predicted anything like the war that occurred. Would the white South have fought for the right to expand slavery had it known that it would sacrifice a quarter of a million of its men in the process? Would the North have fought for the "mystic chords" of a unified nation had it had any idea of the cost in blood? Who could have known that the war would become a war to abolish slavery, immediately, without compensation to slaveholders?

The war could easily have turned out differently, with a different nation-state, with generations more of slavery, with an American apartheid. Yet we tend to talk of the South for generations beforehand as if it knew the toll it was going to extract from the nation;

we equate The North with The Union for generations beforehand, as if New England had not threatened to leave the nation before Southerners considered such a move. In other words, Americans have grown far too comfortable with the Civil War, lulled into assuming its inevitability and its outcome, granting it a moral purpose it assumed only gradually and against the will of many who fought for the Union. We look back on the South's secession as a violation of the natural order, of the way things had to be, but one does not have to be a Dixiecrat to realize that the defeat of the Old South is often used to glorify the current nation-state, to sanctify America's destiny, to suggest the divine favor we enjoy, to show that, through blood, we overcame the original sin of this country. It is too simple a story, both for the North and for the South.[23]

Many white Southerners have wanted to have it both ways: to be staunch Americans, proud of the nation-state, and to be true Southerners, unashamed of their forefathers' rebellion. They have not found it that hard to do. The process began early. As much as white Southerners believed in their right to secede, the identities of Confederate and American proved to be surprisingly easy for most people to reconcile once the war was over. A nationalism that had been constructed on the spot, imagined, could be easily dismantled. Even diehard Southerners could see their dual loyalties. An old Confederate who lived in Atlanta during Reconstruction taunted the Union soldiers on the street. "You may have won the war," he'd say, "but we sure whipped your ass at Chickamauga." The irate soldiers hauled him to their commander, who berated the old man and made him swear out a loyalty oath to the United States of America. The next day, the old man was back at his post on the street. When the Union soldiers walked by, he was ready. "We may have won the war," he yelled, "but the Rebels sure whipped our ass at Chickamauga!" This was a forced convolution, of course, but white Southerners have willingly performed similar ideological gymnastics ever since Appomattox.[24]

The Confederate flag embodies the ambiguity. For some white Southerners, no other symbol seems as rich with meaning. When pressed to explain that meaning, some defenders speak in inarticulate and deeply felt terms of heritage, of great-great-grandfathers, of rights, of hypocritical Yankees, in language with no power to persuade anyone who does not already agree with them. When they speak of slavery, they speak of it only to deny that it had anything at all to do with the war, refusing to accept overwhelming evidence that runs counter to their beliefs. To the defenders of the battle flag, to be ashamed of the symbol is to be ashamed of who they are, of who their family has been. It seems a matter of all or nothing, of denying that history changes the meaning of things. To other defenders of the flag, the explicit connection to the past is not essential. They are not certain that they had ancestors who fought in the Civil War, yet they display the flag with even greater frequency and ardor than any Son of the Confederacy (indeed, to the Sons' dismay), for to them the flag is a *rebel* flag. They are often rebels with only a vague cause; the flag is such a multipurpose symbol precisely because it is so vague. It is a sign of resistance to the boss, to Southern yuppies, to the North, to blacks, to liberals, to any kind of political correctness. In their eyes, the rebel flag stands for the same thing that they imagine it stood for in 1861: Leave Me the Hell Alone.

The Confederate flag is a topic of such debate and divisiveness in the South today because it denies all that black and white Southerners shared, because it reduces the South to a one-time and one-sided political identity. The South and the Confederacy covered the same territory and shared a critical part of history, but they have never been synonymous, not even between 1861 and 1865. Yet Confederate symbolism has spread to places that were staunchly Unionist in the Civil War itself. Drive through the mountain counties of the South, even West Virginia, and notice how many Confederate flags you see, how many people imagine a connection with the Confederacy they have no genealogical or geographical right to claim, how many people seize on what is supposedly a discredited symbol of an aborted nationalism. The Confederacy lives on as a potent symbol, its potency coming from its ambiguity and instability of meaning, a meaning that was not unambiguous even in 1861.

That same ambiguity has permitted white Northerners to use the Civil War for another purpose, dubious and simplistic in its own way. Ever since the war, many of them have tended to see themselves as the chosen, the redeemed, the real nation; black freedom seems a good not only for its own sake but as an emblem of a larger national destiny and freedom. This role has served to sanctify the North and the West and to make the South a sink of iniquity, a focus and explanation for what is lacking in the country in general. The Civil War seems to many white non-Southerners to absolve their ancestors from complicity in slavery for the 250 years before Appomattox. It is this willful forgetfulness that gives credence to charges of Northern hypocrisy from diehard defenders of the Confederacy, who insist that slavery was a national crime and not a purely sectional one.

Southern novelists such as William Faulkner have looked the convoluted Southern mythology in the face, trying to see what it might mean (and, ironically, giving it worldwide attention and credence). "Don't you see?" Faulkner's Ike McCaslin yells at a black man in "The Bear." "This whole land, the whole South, is cursed, and all of us who derive from it whom it ever suckled, white and black both, lie under the curse? . . . What corner of Canaan is this?" [25]

A corner of Canaan: that may be as good a description of the South as we are going to get. At its very heart the South has been, and is, a problematic province of Canaan, the land of milk and honey. White Southerners have shared in the national sense of the United States as a peculiarly bountiful, democratic, and idealistic nation but have always understood that they are not quite as bountiful, democratic, or idealistic as their countrymen in other parts of the nation. It is that tension that underlies the centuries-old struggle to explain the South.

Space, along with time, forms the unavoidable contexts in which we live our lives. People *will* think spatially and historically. But we can be more self-conscious about the *way* we think in these dimensions. The categories in which we place things have everything to do with what we take those things to be. Better, it seems, to talk first of concrete things—poverty and power, specific people with specific interests—rather than of a gaseous Southern "culture" or a suspiciously malleable and sanitized "heritage." We need to see the many connections between local and state, local and national, local and international. We need to recognize that structures of economy, ideology, religion, fashion, and politics cut across the South, connecting some individuals with allies and counterparts elsewhere. We need to see both how permeable the boundary between North and South has always been and how regional difference is continually being reinvented across that boundary. We need to recognize how willingly most white people outside the South supported slavery and segregation, how the movement to end Jim Crow grew up among black Southerners before it was impressed as a problem on the rest of the nation.

Southern history is made up of the things that have happened and are happening on this artificially bounded piece of real estate, however contradictory they may have been and remain. Southern history bespeaks a place that is more complicated than the stories we tell about it. Throughout its history, the South has been a place where poverty and plenty have been thrown together in especially jarring ways, where democracy and oppression, white and black, slavery and freedom, have warred. The very story of the South is a story of unresolved identity, unsettled and restless, unsure and defensive. The South, contrary to so many words written in defense and in attack, was not a fixed, known, and unified place but a place of constant movement, struggle, and negotiation.[26]

There is a tendency for Southerners to see time as the enemy, erasing the inscriptions on the land, destroying whatever certain identity the South has ever had. Louis Rubin, a leading commentator on Southern literature, returned to his birthplace, Charleston, South Carolina, only to find the signs of his childhood gone. "On each successive visit to what had once been my home, I found that what had constituted its substance and accidence both had dwindled." He felt that his childhood and his Southern identity were "becoming more and more a matter of absence, loss, and alienation. I was, that is, steadily becoming dispossessed." But Rubin, recognizing the self-centeredness, the selfishness, of such a view, chose to redefine his relation to the South and the changes both he and the region have undergone, seeking "identity in time, not outside it. Its diminution did not represent merely loss, but change, of which I was a part, and which, because it had happened to me in my time, was mine to cherish, . . . proof that I had been and still was alive."[27]

Those people, black and white, who care about their particular

South should take heart from a vision in which regional identity is continuously being replenished even as other forms, older forms, erode and mutate. Anything that has happened and is happening in this corner of the country rightfully belongs to the South's past, whether or not it seems to fit the template of an imagined Southern culture. There is no essence to be denied, no central theme to violate, no role in the national drama to be betrayed. The South is continually coming into being, continually being remade, continually struggling with its pasts.

4 • Region and Reason

Patricia Nelson Limerick

If region had not had reason on its side, then region would not have had much. In the twentieth century, the idea of regionalism has made few pulses race; passion has not been its instant ally. In truth, for much of the last century regionalism's appeal has rested on an exactly opposite property. In times of harried and disorienting change, the theory went, regions stabilized the pulse, slowed down the heartbeat, and made life seem manageable again. If the word *region* had consistently aroused strong emotion, it would have undermined its own promise of a grounded, healing, stable arrangement of loyalties.

Unreasonable emotion had been assigned, meanwhile, to region's bad twin, section. Regions, by this arrangement, unite, while sections divide. Regions can both complement and compliment one another; sections can only compete. Regions have their roots in a warm and hearty connection between distinctive people and distinctive places; sections have their roots in political and economic struggles for dominance. Regions have rounded, soft borders; sections have sharp, clashing edges. Regions coexist; sections cause civil wars. In truth, anyone who becomes an enthusiast for the more appealing member of this pair will eventually have to reckon with the less appealing member, though that is a reckoning I will postpone until the end of this essay.

And yet, for all the differences in the associations they bring to mind, both region and section have been running an equal risk of obsolescence in the late twentieth century. In an era of historical inquiry in which the categories of race, ethnicity, class, and gender have taken center stage, both region and section register as relics and antiques. In the midst of the campaign to write a version of American history that reckons with inequality and injustice and pays attention to the full diversity of the population, region has been auditioning for the part of the most dismissible category of all. Pulses race and pound in debates over ethnic history and gender history. To many scholars, regional history is where one goes for a nap.

My own experience in these matters has been quite different, and behavior so anomalous requires some explanation.[1] Against all the odds, regionalism did excite my passions and accelerate my heartbeat. I never saw regionalism as peripheral to the tensions of ethnicity; on the contrary, I fell into the belief that thinking in regional terms provided the fairest and the most reasoned response to the challenge of American diversity. If one tried to reckon with the whole of American history at once, one saw only an uninstructive blur, a jangle of unrelated parts. But region permitted one to adjust and train one's vision in a way that uncovered connections, ties, and relations. With particular people in particular places brought into focus, one could build one's units of generalization outward, from place to subregion to region to nation to hemisphere to planet. With region as the key transitional category, the blur began to sort itself out.

When one was paying attention to these more manageable units of understanding, ethnic diversity simply had to get its full recognition. A close look at the history of a particular place could not, I believed, be an exclusive look. Whatever impact they may or may not have had on the Constitution or on Congress, everybody—Indians, Mexican Americans, Asian Americans, whites of all backgrounds—did have an impact on the place where they lived. With all their variations of power and status, all groups had to be written into the stories of place, subregion, and region.[2] To my mind, that mandate for inclusiveness gave regionalism its reason to be.

This premise did not make a world of sense to every person who watched me embrace it. Ethnicity, after all, was no consistent respecter of regional boundaries. Mexican American settlement in Chicago went off the screen of trans-Mississippi regional significance but still remained an important part of Mexican American history. Chinatown in New York was, and is, as important in Asian American studies as Chinatown in San Francisco. By virtue of the border with Mexico and the Pacific Coast, the trans-Mississippi West remained the major area of entry for Mexican and Asian immigrants, but the region did not retain an exclusive hold on the stories of these people. Conversations with scholars of color thus drove me back to the question, Why did I care so much about region? How, if at all, were the causes of regional inclusiveness and ethnic inclusiveness joined together?

I placed all my cards on the table in the last lines of *The Legacy of Conquest*, and I will confess that eight years after writing these words their earnest hopefulness makes me wince. "Indians, Hispanics, Asians, blacks, Anglos, businesspeople, workers, politicians, bureaucrats, natives, and newcomers, we share the same region and its history," I wrote in 1986, "but we wait to be introduced. The serious exploration of the process that made us neighbors provides that introduction."[3] Here, without anything much in the way of a veil or disguise, was my reason for embracing regional history: I thought it would make us better neighbors. I thought regionalism would curtail the inclination of some Westerners to dismiss other Westerners as aliens and outsiders. With a shared Western past laid out before us, I thought, regional identity could provide the cultural and social loom to knit a fragmented society together. Both reason and hope coincided in this common cause, I thought.

Others in my company showed at least moments of receptivity to this hope. I remember in particular a meeting of the senior seminar on regionalism that I taught in the fall of 1977. I had asked the students to read what I thought were ringing statements of conviction by the American regionalists of the 1930s.[4] They had not, however, rung for the students. The readings and the students' souls had clearly stayed in separate spheres, even separate time zones. While I tried to tug them into discussion, the students gave me the eloquent look mastered by every undergraduate. "We are, of course, your powerless captives," that look says. "If you want to bore us to death, it is your right, but we *can* see to it that exercising that right will give you no pleasure." If we did not reverse this downward spiral, we faced many weeks of ever-deepening boredom. Regionalism was in trouble, and so was I.

I retreated to the blackboard, asking the students to forget the readings (with this request they were willing to comply) and tell me what they themselves did not like about modern life (this request made them even more enthusiastic). The list covered the board: mass media, mass marketing, mass society, mass alienation; the impersonality, detachment, and coldness of social relations; cynical politics; omnipresent commercialism; disconnected loyalties; ethnic friction, fragmentation, divisiveness, and hostility. Each of these categories came with abundant examples, from Watergate to McDonald's restaurant design, from racial separatism to disco. "*Discontent*," as one student observed, "begins with *disco*."

With this rich and detailed catalogue of irritation on record, the course got a second wind. "You may not have noticed it the first time through," I could now tell the students, "but you and those regionalists have a fair amount in common." They did, in truth, perk up. Whether or not region became their antidote of choice, they understood the concerns that might lead others to that preference.

To a number of observers, this classroom exercise would appear to be simply another unreasoning celebration of antimodernism, another nostalgic attempt to evade the complex and challenging contemporary world. Deployers of the charge of antimodernism, I feel more and more, have their own evasions to address. It is a fact beyond dispute: there are damned good reasons to object to modern life and, for that matter, to postmodern life. Trying to imagine how life might be lived in a more immediate and engaging web of loyalty, tied to the place of one's residence, is more than a psychiatric symptom, more than a sociocultural pathology, more than a confession that one cannot cope with modern times.[5]

For all these reasons, I was an enthusiast for regionalism long before I realized how much my own poor region needed help. Seemingly without consequence or relevance, the history of Western America had been rendered distant and dismissible, an ideal terrain for escapism and fantasy, simply the stage on which the great frontier process had played out its final act.[6] With that framework still fixed in place in the early 1980s, it was not going to be an easy matter to persuade other American historians to take Western places and events seriously. By the same token, it was not going to be easy to liberate those places and events from the unreflecting narrative of the westward movement, a narrative finally as accommodating as a straitjacket.

And yet the stakes in this campaign extended way beyond the area of turf between the Mississippi River and the Pacific coast. More and more, my conviction became this: doing justice to the complexity and reality of Western American history was a vital component of national self-exploration, a component that we had neglected at their peril. A person recovering from the inaccurate images of the West's past was a person recovering from some of the worst distortions afflicting American history in general. If one recognized, for instance, that the trans-Mississippi West is a significant part of this nation, and recognized the remarkable diversity of its founding populations, one was instantly freed from nostalgia for a lost age of American unity, freed from yearning for a lost wholeness or clarity in American history. Think, for instance, of the comfort and peace that a knowledge of Western American history could bring to a scholar like Arthur Schlesinger Jr.[7] If he put this never very united region at the center of his attention, he could give up grieving over the disuniting of America and explore more interesting emotional and intellectual terrain. The willingness to incorporate the American West fully into one's picture of national history, I was fully convinced by the mid-1980s, operates on the mind like a kind of historiographic chiropractic service. In the mid-1990s I remain convinced by this proposition: taking the West seriously realigns the thinking and removes the kinks of knotted assumptions; it leaves the historian's mind limber, energetic, and ready to take on the challenge of American diversity with good grace.[8]

To my mind, then, regionalism carried the joint appeal of reason and sentiment. I wanted to draw attention to the wider and deeper national lesson that comes when the borders of historical significance are truly expanded to the Pacific. Sentiment did request more of an assertion of an intrinsic Western significance, but reason overruled that request. Reason would not vote for the proposition that because some events happened between the Pacific and the Mississippi, they were by the stark fact of their occurrence made significant. My colleague in Western American history Donald Worster mocked this notion of intrinsic regional significance as heartily as it deserved to be mocked: "Undoubtedly," he wrote, "the history of the West is important to those who live here, in the same way the history of Tibet is important to Tibetans or the role of a first grader in the school play is interesting to his mother or father. But why should anyone living elsewhere pay any attention to the West? Does it hold some significance for the nation and the world, and if it does, what is it?"[9]

Worster's uncomfortable remarks remind every regionalist that while the assertion "It's important because it's *our* story" might have some power to rally fellow provincials, it does not do much good to convert the unconverted, even under the best of circumstances. And in the mid-1980s circumstances were not at their best; persuasion was an even more challenging undertaking in an era of much grumpiness on the part of many American historians who already saw a crisis of synthesis, as American history stretched to contain the variables of race, class, ethnicity, and gender. Adding one more variable to that list might well seem to be adding the straw that would take care of the camel's back. But adding the concept of region, I believed, actually made the project of national synthesis more grounded and more manageable.

Why did I see a region where others saw only another interchangeable part of a homogenized nation-state? Over the years I sorted out my "top ten" reasons for treating the West as a region, defining it with flexible borders at the Pacific and at the hundredth meridian, where rainfall drops below the twenty inches a year needed to sustain agriculture. This West is not, heaven knows, a unit of homogeneity and internal consistency. But much of this territory shares common characteristics, characteristics that do not appear in every part of the West but overlap in enough Western places to give the whole some conceptual unity. In all these characteristics, my hope for a regionalism in which environmental history provided a foundation for an interwoven ethnic history should be obvious.

1. The West is more prone than other regions to aridity and semiaridity, and this is a fact full of consequence, because most of what Anglo-Americans considered (and consider) normal in a landscape requires much more water than the West would provide. The scarcity of water inspired a distinctive regional campaign to change nature: to build—with heavy support from the federal government—a vast network of dams, reservoirs, and canals to "normalize" this anomalous landscape.[10]

2. The West contains more Indian reservations, and more visible, unvanished Indian people. I do not mean to lessen the significance of the Mohawk people, or the Eastern Cherokees, or the Pequots. I am not making any claim here for the West's uniqueness, but simply saying that the center of gravity in American Indian affairs is in the West, with the bulk of the land in the United States that is still under tribal sovereignty and with the majority of the descendants of the conquered people.[11]

3. The West shares a border with Mexico and has been the entry point for Mexican immigrants. People immigrating from Mexico have not had to cross an ocean, and the relationship between immigrant and home country has thus been substantially different from other forms of American immigration. Moreover, the conditions of the border between Mexico and America have been distinctive and remarkable; it is a place where a prosperous, developed nation shares a land connection with an underdeveloped, Third World nation. Equally important, much of the West was once under the sovereignty of Spain and then Mexico, and acquired in a clear war of conquest against another nation. Originally participants in an invasion and conquest of Indian territory, Spanish-speaking people thus came to share with Indian people the status of a minority by conquest, their rights theoretically guaranteed by international treaty.[12]

4. The West borders on the Pacific. The West was thus tied to the nation by maritime connections as well as by overland connections; it was and is the entry point for Asian immigration; it was the center and staging ground of anti-Asian agitation. It is the focal point for the shift in the balance of American trade, and perhaps in the shift of American diplomatic relations, from Europe to Asia.[13]

5. The West contains the bulk of the U.S. land still under federal

control. The Eastern states privatized the public domain, and privatized it *fast.* The Western states followed another track entirely, in part because the aridity, or sometimes the elevation, of much Western land made it unsuitable for conventional Anglo-American economic development and in part because the federal government made a decisive swing toward permanent ownership of the public domain, beginning with the creation of the Forest Reserves in 1891.[14]

6. Largely as a consequence of the public lands and relations with conquered people, the West has provided a particularly illuminating case study in state power, in showing how the United States as a nation conducted conquest. In the permanent control of public lands, in the subsidizing of private businesses like the railroad, in the construction of federal dams, in the reckoning of the treaty rights of Indian people, as well as the rights awarded Mexican people under the Treaty of Guadalupe-Hidalgo, the operations of the federal government are spotlit. In many ways, the Department of the Interior began as, and continued to be, a special state agency for the governance of the West. Any discussion of the powers of the federal government—or of public culture, to use Thomas Bender's phrase—that does not include this distinctive regional relationship will be incomplete to the point of serious distortion.[15] In Western history one can see the growth and shaping of federal power long before the more conventionally recognized periods of federal growth, the Progressive Era and the New Deal. As Richard White puts it, "While the federal government shaped the West, however, the West itself served as the kindergarten of the American state. . . . In the West, federal power took on modern forms."[16]

7. The West has a particularly dramatic, though certainly not unique, long-term involvement with the boom-and-bust economies of extractive industries (mining, logging, ranching, oil drilling, and commercial farming), whose cycles of prosperity the federal government has sometimes moderated but never tamed.[17]

8. The West has an equally long-term involvement with commercial, intentional mythologizing of the West as a place of romantic escape and adventure. Here, again, regional history makes direct contact with Thomas Bender's call for a synthesis hinged on an exploration of public culture. Explore American public culture

without a consideration of Western mythologizing, and you have a synthesis with a major part left out. This mythologizing has, indeed, created a nearly intractable dilemma in regional and national self-knowledge. The popularizing of the Western image has given the region a particularly heavy dependence on the uncertain industry of tourism and on the effort to meet the expectations generated by the mythmakers.[18]

9. Despite the heavy dose of treacle in the romantic image of the West, the region has a long history as the nation's dumping ground, either for troubling populations of Indians or Mormons or for toxic and radioactive substances. Aridity produced the wide open spaces so basic to the mythic appeal of the West; the same factor kept many areas sparsely inhabited and thus identified them as leading candidates for disposal of substances not compatible with human settlement. Deserts, moreover, struck Anglo-Americans as wastelands to begin with; a little radioactive contamination could hardly hurt an area known, from the beginning, for its desolation. It was, for instance, surely no surprise to anyone when all the finalists for permanent national nuclear waste dump were in the West.[19]

10. As a result of a number of these factors, the West is particularly prone to demonstrate the unsettled aspects of conquest, to show in the late twentieth century more than its share of the evidence that the conquest of North America came to no clear point of completion. From the presence of the majority of the conquered people, and the unresolved status of their rights, to the ways in which aridity refuses to mask the impact of conquest, leaving everything from abandoned mines to the effects of erosion exposed and unmistakable, the West displays the ongoing legacy of conquest in everyday life.

As persuasive as I may find this list, presenting this definition of the West as a region often evoked a compelling instinct in listeners or readers to take it apart. This was, some argued, a definition of region that rested heavily on hindsight, on knowing how things turned out. The Navajo lived at the center of the universe, not in "the West"; Spanish settlements in New Mexico were part of *el norte*, not of "the West." The very idea of Western American history has as its prerequisite a fairly recently developed awareness of the West as a unit of thought and study, an awareness that has tried to wrap itself around the history that occurred before that unit came into consciousness.

Hindsight of this sort is, however, omnipresent in the definition of historical fields. Reading American history textbooks is, in fact, a prolonged encounter with texts structured around hindsight. At their origin, the British Atlantic colonies seemed very separate indeed, but foreknowledge of the fact that they would coalesce into a union causes the textbook writers to treat the colonies as a unit. No one in the 1840s could predict with certainty the onset of the Civil War, but foreknowledge of the war structures the texts, following antebellum issues as they build to the explosion of war. Western regionalism is just as much a product of hindsight, and the most important components of that hindsight are changes from the last three decades: the rise of environmentalism; the change in the principal sources of immigration, from Europe to Asia and Latin America; and the shift in the population in the mid-1980s, when the population of the West and the South came to outnumber that of the Midwest and Northeast. On these counts, and no doubt others, Western regional history has been a construction of hindsight, and on that count it is remarkably similar to the constructions governing the rest of American history.

Others observed that my list of factors did not describe all parts of the West with equal accuracy. This objection was often delivered in the form of the comment that the coastal Pacific Northwest is awfully *wet* for inclusion in a region otherwise defined by aridity. This is certainly true, but the argument, again, was that the West holds together, not because each and every one of these factors appears in every place, but because a number of them coincide and overlap. Coastal Oregon and Washington are quite wet, although interior Oregon and Washington are semi-deserts. Moreover, coastal Washington registers high on other Western variables: it has a significant Indian presence, with considerable agitation recently over the reassertion of Indian fishing rights; it has lots of federally controlled land; the Columbia River basin has been a central arena of federal dam building; the logging business of the Pacific Northwest shows the Western boom-and-bust economy at its starkest; the area is deeply involved in Pacific basin issues. We may have lost the Pacific Northwest on the basis of aridity, but we re-gained it on four or five other variables.

Until we have reckoned with the West, the journalist and histo-rian Charles Howard Shinn wrote in 1884, "we have learned only a part of the lesson that America has to teach."[20] Each of the ten characteristics in my regional list, brought to a focus in the West, has enormous national significance. Whether it is a matter of the growth of federal power or the unsettled issues of conquest, these are clearly topics of national or even international concern. Indeed, one of the more puzzling objections to Western regionalism in the last few years has been the assertion that thinking of the West as a region marginalizes the West and cancels out the national signifi-cance of regional events. On the contrary, local history can inhabit, at one and the same time, regional, national, and planetary levels of significance. Without the regional level of meaning, the more general levels are unrooted, ungrounded, abstract, and uncon-vincing.

In two areas in particular, Western regional history has made an essential contribution to national history: in the history of race relations and in environmental history. The pattern of Western race relations has been considerably more complex than the pattern of race relations in the East. In the West one had to add enormous tribal diversity (a greater diversity than in the Eastern United States), Spanish colonization, and Mexican and Asian immigration to the usual picture of American race relations as hinged on an axis of encounters between blacks and whites, African Americans and Anglo-Americans. Confronted by the populations in the West, white Americans there had no comfortable and predictable ranking of race to fall back on. Where was the hierarchy that could sort out Western Indians (Pueblo, Lakota, Modoc, Paiute, Pima, Coman-che, Salish, Pawnee, etc., *plus* many of the Eastern tribes, Chero-kee, Choctaw, Chickasaw, Creek, Seminole, made into Western refugees), established Hispano residents, recent Mexican immi-grants, Chinese immigrants, Japanese immigrants, Filipino immi-grants, African Americans, European ethnics, and, perhaps the most puzzling ethnicity of all, Utah Mormons? Where was the ra-cial hierarchy that could put that swirl of people into some sort of clear order? Perhaps I exaggerate the clarity and simplicity of East-

ern race relations in drawing this comparison. But these things are
relative, and the Western situation was, in truth, more complex
and muddled.

One could not do justice to the story of American race relations
without giving the trans-Mississippi West its full share of attention.
And in the same spirit, historians of the human relationship to the
physical environment had to give full attention to the West. Here
we confronted a difference of historiographical contingency more
than a difference of real content. For a time, Western historians
had nearly exclusive custody of environmental history. Because so
much of Western settlement and development hinged on the extraction of natural resources, because much of the Western landscape is indeed grand and striking, because the institutional behavior of National Parks and National Forests gave a concrete focus to
the question of attitudes toward nature, Western historians paid
attention to the reciprocal relations between humans and their natural environments before historians of many other areas did. This
was an undeserved advantage; environmental history was never
really the exclusive property of any region. Still, at a time when
Western history did not seem to have much else going for it, it was
hard to give up this advantage, deserved or not. In recent years
Easterners have begun to show up at Western water conferences;
by virtue of pollution, the residents of the East have created for
themselves the condition of water scarcity, a condition that has
long characterized the West. The environmental history of the
West, sometimes to the regret of Easterners, becomes more relevant to the whole nation every day.

It was reasonable to argue that American history would be incomplete until it reckoned with topics brought to a focus in the
West, and it was reasonable to argue that regional history could
help in the cause of synthesizing American history, reversing the
fragmentation of the field that many have lamented. Region crosses
the other boundaries and divisions. In the West, for instance, region took the disparate stories of Indian tribes, Hispanic villages,
Anglo-American pioneer settlements, and Asian American immigrant communities and pulled them into one story, as these various
groups interacted in the big process of the invasion and conquest
of the region. Region took, as well, men's stories and women's

stories and found their areas of overlap. Region, in other words, permitted an unexpected approach to the seemingly intractable divisions of history, a way to find, quite literally, common ground in seemingly detached and separate narratives.

When historians fell into the habit of lamenting the hard times on which narrative history had fallen, we lamented the loss of one particular narrative: the kind of narrative structured around one subject—a group of people who are central on the opening pages, in the middle, and at the end. What we have before us now is a much more interesting kind of narrative, more of a Dickensian narrative. This is not necessarily a weaker sort of story. It is instead a story in which a bunch of *very* unrelated people are separately introduced, and then, not necessarily with any great speed, they move toward one another. By the last third or so of the story they are all entangled in one another's lives; they have met, fallen in love, quarreled, stolen from or murdered one another. Even though their stories began very separately, they end up interwoven in a way that will not let them ever again be detached from one another.

Region, then, becomes one strand in the converging and entangling of these narratives. Colonial history, for instance, can and should have a number of narrative origins, with Spanish colonial New Mexico and Spanish colonial Texas as points of origin along with British colonial Virginia and British colonial Massachusetts. Just as Virginia and Massachusetts began with very different origins but then merged into the same story, so did New Mexico and Texas eventually arrive as significant parts of the Union. Since historians are permitted to be considerably more flatfooted narrators than novelists, the historian does not have to hold these narratives suspended apart from one another until events bring them together. On the contrary, the historian can hop from west to east and east to west, comparing and contrasting what colonial life meant in its varied settings. The narrative construction "meanwhile, back at the ranch," never impressed anyone with its artfulness, but it did serve to hold plots together.

We can, then, take our inspiration from Dickens's narrative structure of people beginning with diverse origins and in seemingly separate plots and then moving into a common story. We can, as well, celebrate the pleasures and advantages of hindsight, letting it provide the narrative coherence we think we have lost. Acquired by forcible conquest, California, Arizona, New Mexico, and Texas now function as part of the Union, and the story of their arrival in the Union can be as compelling and coherent as the story of arrival for the thirteen Atlantic colonies.

Until we write this Dickensian, multi-origin story of the Union, the whole we have called "American history" remains very much a fragment itself. Most American historians, including all the writers of college-level American history textbooks, have postponed their reckoning with the Western half of the nation.[21] With region as one of our principal categories of historical investigation, the basic narrative of American history gains a new flexibility and range. The South, the Northeast, the Midwest, and the West can become the foundation for this more complex narrative.

And yet, to many historians, region is a foundation matching the marshmallow in its structural firmness. Regions, to their historiographic peril, do not seem altogether real. When they are examined, inspected, and appraised for their solidity, permanence, consistency, and authenticity, regions behave very much as the wicked Witch of the West did when the bucket of water hit her. While geography plays a role in their definition, regions are much more the creations of human thought and behavior than they are the products of nature. At first encounter, this proposition does indeed seem to cause the region to melt away before one's eyes.

When I first heard the argument that Edward Ayers presents in his essay here, I had a glimpse of how the Witch of the West might have felt in the moment before meltdown. For twenty years the field of Western American history has been trying to catch up to Southern history in a variety of ways, particularly in that field's serious attention to race relations. Western historians have been puffing along, trying to match the depth, intensity, and seriousness of Southern history. As we finally closed the distance between the fields, one of the first voices we heard was Ayers's energetic voice calling out not "welcome!" or "congratulations!" but a warning that the South's regional distinctiveness, difference, purity, and authenticity had been much exaggerated. So high was this level of variation and contingency in its characteristics that the South as a clearly defined, bounded, and consistent region did not exist.

My first response was a clear and simple one: "The South," I felt I had to say to Ayers, "had *better* exist anyway, because Western historians have been directing an awful lot of our time and energy into following the example of Southern historians." But with this response, I was only adding one more piece to a big stack of evidence that Western American historians have been slow to face up to cultural and literary theory. For all our differences of emphasis and interpretation, we have been a pretty prosaic-minded bunch, reluctant to embrace the proposition that human experience and human categories are matters of construction and invention. The attention of Western historians has been focused on resolutely material topics: beaver pelts, wagons, mines, railroad tracks, cattle, farm equipment, dams, ditches, crops, oil pumps, sawmills, military bases, defense plants, freeways, suburbs. We may have spent part of the late twentieth century dividing into camps of Old Western Historians and New (increasingly, Middle-Aged) Western Historians, but a striking percentage of both Old and New Western Historians have invested little time or attention in theoretical or methodological self-consciousness.

I, personally, poured all the linguistic and theoretical energy I had into one cause, namely, questioning the clarity and meaning of the word *frontier*. Indeed, it has been my principal career achievement to make quite a number of historians flinch when, in my company, they use the f-word without a careful definition. Having unleashed a small epidemic of queasiness over one term, however, I returned to the traditions of Western historians and freely used many other, equally questionable terms with unself-conscious, untheoretical ease.[22]

Indeed, watching other historians take "the linguistic turn," recasting everything that we used to call "events" into "constructions" and "discourses," I have played the part of something close to a reactionary myself. I find myself, for instance, imagining a scenario, in the fairly immediate future, of a completely silent humanities classroom building. "Why, no one's here!" one would think, but then, when one looked into the classrooms, one would find a full complement of students, silent in their chairs. In front of each class would stand a professor, also speechless. What spell had been cast on these buildings? The professors would have tried to begin their lectures. "This is a course," one of them might have begun, "in United States history, though the appropriateness of organizing knowledge by the boundaries of the nation-state is currently very much in dispute. Indeed, the very term *history* carries no clear meaning at all. What we once complacently called history proves to be the shifting product of manipulations of power and contests for legitimation. So perhaps 'United States history' is not really a workable name for this course, but if I don't call it that, I don't really know what I *could* call it."

And thus it would go, classroom by classroom, as each lecturer ran aground on the complicated sandbars and shoals of current language. I am not, let me make clear, sketching a scenario in "political correctness." Sensitivity to the feelings of categorized people is only one element—and to my mind, quite a legitimate element—of how we have been made self-conscious about our language. Beyond any individual's personal sensitivity, every central term of historical discussion—*nation, race, ethnicity, gender, power, agency, victimization, oppression, privilege, justice, equality, cause, effect, frontier, conquest, South, North, Midwest, West*—is complex and treacherous, loaded with contradictions and multiple meanings and confusion. It is perfectly reasonable to question and interrupt the carefree use of these terms. But it is also reasonable to worry about the obstacles now placed in the path of communication. People engaged in particular tasks need tools: carpenters need hammers and levels and saws; cooks need spoons and pots and measuring cups; lecturers need words, words they can use without first putting themselves and their audience through prolonged fits of definitional anxiety.

Thus speaks the prosaic-minded Western historian, anxious to return home to that realm of material things—mines, logs, saddles, oil pumps, tractors—that has so long given this field its ballast. And yet, often against our will, we Western historians have been forced to face the fact that the concept of a region called the West is *not* a well-established, universally recognized fact sitting out there, awaiting discovery, in verifiable, objective, tangible reality. This region comes heavily endowed with myths, dreams, and stereotypes. Trying to understand the West requires an unending struggle with a narrow, essential definition by which *Western* means the Bonanza Ranch and *Westerner* means a handsome white man on horseback. Moreover, whether we like it or not, Western historians live lives punctuated by the question, "Is there *really* a West, and wasn't it once West of Jamestown, or West of Plymouth?" If Worcester, Massachusetts, or Winchester, Virginia, were once someone's West, the implication of this question seems to be, then New Mexico, Oregon, and Idaho are now, somehow or other, not entirely real.

New Mexico, Oregon, and Idaho have, nonetheless, been hanging tough, refusing to melt away whether or not they are permitted the right to occupy a regional unit. But as the names of these considerably different, noninterchangeable states indicate, the places that could now occupy the category "American West" vary a great deal in history, politics, culture, and economy. Southern historians, Ayers argues persuasively, have every reason to reject the idea of a solid South with a settled, distinctive culture. In those terms, the advantage of the Western historian may well be this: no one has ever made a convincing case that the various residents of the area have shared a common world-view, a common set of values, a common framework of custom. Southern historians may have to be reminded that their region is more complicated than conventional historical handling makes it seem. Western historians have—and sometimes this is to our sorrow—a region that was never anything but complicated and internally disharmonious. Accordingly, references to "the West" will always cause someone to ask, "What did you mean by *that?*"

The word *West,* I am more and more willing to admit, is finally a piece of national common property whose use and ownership have to be closely regulated, structured, and overseen by a negotiated agreement in joint custody. When it is in Peter Onuf's custody, the West will live in Ohio. When it is in my custody, the West will live between the Pacific and the hundredth meridian. When it is in Edward Ayers's custody, the West may well occupy the position of an awkward third party, sitting by while the North and the South work out their complicated relationship. *West,* like every other contested term of its kind, will have to make its peace with the treatment given to it by its various custody holders. More important, the various custody holders will have to make their peace with one another rather than trying to put forward an exclusive claim to legitimate and authentic ownership.

Dollar for dollar, few of those who hold a stake in the word *West* have done a more effective job of cashing in on their investment than Roy Rogers, Western actor and singer. In a recent song, Roy Rogers has a moment of full, postmodernist, theoretical self-consciousness. The song is called "Alive and Kickin'," and it hinges on Roy's feeling that he has "grown up with everybody who's alive and kickin' today." Addressing the several generations of his audience, Roy offers this moment of self-analysis: "If it wasn't for you," he says, "there wouldn't be no me."[23] The cowboy singer Roy Rogers, as the person who operates under that name apparently realizes, is a construction, an invention, and a collaboration between and among moviegoer, actor, producer, advertiser, retail marketer, musician, and fan. "If it wasn't for you, there wouldn't be no me" is a fine slogan for this whole regional story. If it wasn't for the North, there wouldn't be no South. If it wasn't for unionists, there wouldn't be no disunionists; if it wasn't for the Federalists, there wouldn't be no sectionalists. If it wasn't for the permanence of the Union and the federal government, there wouldn't be no West. If it wasn't for the core, there wouldn't be no periphery. If it wasn't for an East Coast–centered mainstream American history, there wouldn't be no regional self-assertion.

If Western historians had resisted the lead of Roy Rogers and tried to hold out and deny the relevance of cultural theory, the events of the 1990s would have made that evasion impossible. In 1992 President William Jefferson Clinton set the stage for a new and instructive performance of regionalism. The appointment of Bruce Babbitt as secretary of the interior had big ramifications for the management of the Western public lands. Low fees for grazing on the public lands, a mining law left over from 1872 that virtually gives away minerals, the subordination of the value of wildlife habitat to the value of logging, federal subsidies for irrigation and power development—various customs and practices that had become the norm in relations between the federal government and the West were now open to reconsideration.

Miners, cattle raisers, loggers, and farmers instantly launched into a regional project of image construction, financed in part by the major resource-extracting corporations. Secretary Babbitt, they said, had declared a "War on the West."[24] The West that the Secretary attacked and that the resource users would defend, these regional patriots said, was the Real West, the individualistic West of hardy men and women working closely with nature, with characters honed to a self-reliant edge by the constant tests of endurance and ingenuity intrinsic to their outdoor occupations.

"The War on the West"? Postmodernist patterns of construction and performance were instantly uncovered here by the follow-up question, asked by a surprising number of newspaper reporters: "The war on *which* West?" By the 1990s the trans-Mississippi West had accumulated at least two decades of status as the nation's most urbanized region.[25] Quite a number of those urban Westerners thought that the area's greatest attraction was the recreational opportunities in the wide open spaces. Miners, ranchers, farmers, and loggers were a tiny minority of the Western population. Hikers, skiers, hunters, fishers, weekend tourists, and voters who simply preferred the idea of preservation to the idea of extraction had come to outnumber the conventional resource users. In the minds of that recreation-oriented group, Secretary Babbitt was waging a "War *for* the West," not *on* it.

The urbanites may have had numbers of their side, but they played with one great disadvantage: by the conventional images of the West in popular culture, the ranchers looked like the real Westerners, with real legitimacy, with real *pedigree*. For most of the twentieth century, if one had staged a round of the old game show "To Tell the Truth," assigning the panel the task of guessing which person—a rancher or an office worker with a fondness for weekend hiking—was the *real* Westerner, the panelists would have gotten it in an instant. Appearance would have given all the clues. The panel could have guessed the winning answer without going to the trouble to ask any questions.

And yet, in the mid-1990s such a panel would have to go back

and ask the questions. Assumptions about Western identity are up
for reexamination. Is Bruce Babbitt the enemy of the Real and Rural West or the champion of the Real and Urban West? Even the
category "urban West" deserves a close reexamination on the axis
of class, since it includes many urban people in poverty to whom
outdoor recreation is irrelevant. Since Babbitt was born in Arizona
and raised on a ranch, his own identity is a major element of the
confusion here; his pedigree and his policies seem dramatically,
remarkably at odds.

As Secretary Babbitt maneuvered through minefields of regional
imagery, as shots in the battle over Western identity flew in all
directions, these abstract matters of cultural construction became
all too actual and consequential. Would it console the secretary of
the interior to know that he has inherited two centuries of heated
rhetoric and anxious behavior around the fault line where Section
meets Union? Every time the secretary visits a Western location,
the protesters are there to denounce him as a federal fiend engaged
in sectional warfare, destroying the noblest heritage of this region.
Would it be any comfort to the secretary, when he is denounced
as the enemy of the West, to know that regions are constructions
and inventions?

The human mind plays the essential role in the creation, construction, and maintenance of regions. Whatever powers this proposition has to soothe the minds of those engaged in changing federal policy, the idea turns out, rather to my surprise, to soothe me.
When Edward Ayers and Peter Onuf made this argument at Johns
Hopkins in 1993, I did my best to mock it. It seemed to me that
saying that region was an act of mind carried the corollary "Therefore region is not real." To say that a region was constructed or
invented, I thought, was to say that a region was not actual or
consequential. In slipping into this assumption, I traveled with a
fairly sizable group of the prosaic-minded, who assume that events
that occur in the human mind are separated from events that occur
in physical reality. If regions are mental constructions, it seemed to
us at first, then regions are not real.

It does not, I was surprised to discover, take a world of effort to
recover from this notion. Humans thought of union, and, as Peter
Onuf tells us, they thought of section as the opposite condition that

threatened union. They then wrote a constitution that recorded those structures of thought. Over the decades, because of those mental acts, came federally sponsored Indian wars, federally sponsored land distribution, and a federally sponsored war to suppress both the idea and the practice of disunion. Because of an idea of the South and of Southernness, people have submitted to federal authority and resisted federal authority; they have stayed home and moved away; they have stood in solidarity and stood in one another's way; they have killed and been killed. Region is a mental act and region is real, at one and the same time. If Westerners from Roy Rogers to Bruce Babbitt are at last reckoning with this paradoxical fact, then it would be awkward for me to linger too far behind.

If Secretary of Interior Bruce Babbitt has not been able to avoid region's evil twin section, then neither can I. From my first encounter with it, region appealed to me because it seemed to be a tool of inclusion, a device that could draw a thread across the gaps and tears left by ethnic tensions and friction. The Federalists feared disunion and saw section as union's principal threat; as a minor footnote to that story two centuries later, I feared disunion and saw region as union's principal ally. There is, I realize, considerable irony in my curious ability to see a device for union in what has also been, under the name *section*, the most effective device for disunion this nation has ever seen. This irony is only made worse by current, international stories of regional rivalry; simply the invocation of the phrase "Eastern Europe" might make anyone swear off an enthusiasm for regional identity for life.

The former Yugoslavia, however, did not set the model or the norm for regionalism, any more than the former Confederacy did. Humans, with all their various techniques of construction and invention, have an endless array of choices in defining and shaping regional identification and loyalty, with an equally endless range in degrees of friction and violence. And yet for all the cheer in that observation, the lesson of sectional and regional friction provides an important warning against a foolish cheer in these matters.

Ten years ago, by sheer will, I was able to see in region a form of loyalty and identification that could cross over the barriers of race, ethnicity, gender, and, most astonishing, class. Now I strain to see even the outlines of that vision of union through region, or through anything else. I return, more than I would like to, to the memory of a conversation with the professor who taught my freshman course in Western civilization. Jasper Rose was British, eccentric, and given to the use of terms like *ducky*. In the discussion of the Reformation, Mr. Rose spoke—all too persuasively, it seemed to me—about the doctrine of original sin. Could my kind and knowledgeable professor actually believe that there was a darkness implanted in the souls of human beings, a kink in their character that put harmony and peace out of their reach?

"Mr. Rose," I said after class, "when you talked about human depravity, it sounded like you believe that there *is* such a thing. You surely don't believe in that, do you?"

Mr. Rose looked at me, and it is very clear to me now that he saw a seventeen-year-old who was going to fight reality, and fight it hard.

"Just wait, ducky," he said. "Just wait."

When the idea of region seemed to have the support of both reason and emotion, and when the unifying idea of region overpowered the divisive idea of section, I held Mr. Rose's warning at bay. Region was, admittedly, an odd antidote for the disheartening effects of the record of human friction, disunion, and cruelty. For all its peculiarity, and despite my continued affection for it, region finally matches most other intellectual antidotes and curatives in the unevenness of its performance. It neither worked for everyone, nor worked for very long. Reason requests another approach, which neither reason nor passion has been quick to supply.

Notes

Introduction

1. For useful overviews see Richard Maxwell Brown, "The New Regionalism in America, 1970–1981," in *Regionalism and the Pacific Northwest*, ed. William G. Robbins, Robert J. Frank, and Richard E. Ross (Corvallis: Oregon State University Press, 1983), 37–96; and Michael Steiner and Clarence Mondale, eds., *Region and Regionalism in the United States: A Source Book for the Humanities and Social Sciences* (New York: Garland, 1988).

2. John Shelton Reed is an exception to this generalization about sociological perspectives on region, for he emphasizes the role of events in changing regional self-perception. See his entry "Southerners" in *Harvard Encyclopedia of American Ethnic Groups*, ed. Stephan Thernstrom (Cambridge: Harvard University Press, 1980), 944–48.

3. These include Joyce Appleby, *Capitalism and a New Social Order: The Republican Vision of the 1790s* (New York: New York University Press, 1984); Jack P. Greene, *Peripheries and Center: Constitutional Development in the Extended Polities of the British Empire and the United States, 1607–1788* (Athens: University of Georgia Press, 1986), *Pursuits of Happiness: The Social Development of Early Modern British Colonies and the Formation of American Culture* (Chapel Hill: University of North Carolina Press, 1988), and *The Intellectual Construction of America: Exceptionalism and Identity from 1492 to 1800* (Chapel Hill: University of North

Carolina Press, 1993); and Gordon S. Wood, *The Radicalism of the American Revolution* (New York: Knopf, 1992).

4. For a good introduction to the historiography see Jack P. Greene and J. R. Pole, eds., *Colonial British America: Essays in the New History of the Early Modern Era* (Baltimore: Johns Hopkins University Press, 1984), 1–17. The most ambitious recent effort to establish connections between distinctive British emigrations and colonial settlement regions is David Hackett Fischer, *Albion's Seed: Four British Folkways in America* (New York: Oxford University Press, 1989). A "Forum" on Fischer's book may be found in *William and Mary Quarterly*, 3rd ser., 48 (1991), 260–308. See also D. W. Meinig, *The Shaping of America: A Geographical Perspective of Five Hundred Years of History*, vol. 1, *Atlantic America, 1492–1800* (New Haven: Yale University Press, 1986). Greene discusses both Fischer and Meinig in "Interpretive Frameworks: The Quest for Intellectual Order in Early American History," *William and Mary Quarterly* 48 (1991), 515–30. Greene elaborates a common developmental model for the various settlement areas of Anglo-America that minimizes regional distinctiveness in *Pursuits of Happiness.* "During the generations following the American Revolution," Greene writes, "the southern states rapidly became not just a *distinctive* but, at least on the issue of its inhabitants' continuing commitment to chattel slavery, a *deviant* section of American society. . . . An enhanced sense of the differences between North and South [was only] developed and articulated . . . after 1820" (Greene, *Pursuits of Happiness,* 1). This theme is further developed in Greene, "The Constitution of 1787 and the Question of Southern Distinctiveness," in Greene, *Imperatives, Behaviors, and Identities: Essays in Early American Cultural History* (Charlottesville: University Press of Virginia, 1992), 327–47.

5. The key text in this literature is Bernard Bailyn, *The Ideological Origins of the American Revolution* (Cambridge: Harvard University Press, 1967). For historiographical context see Daniel T. Rodgers, "Republicanism: The Career of a Concept," *Journal of American History* 79 (1992), 11–38.

6. The phrase is borrowed from Benedict Anderson, *Imagined Communities: Reflections on the Origin and Spread of Nationalism,* rev. ed. (London: Verso, 1991). For further references to the literature on nationalism generally and American nationality in particular, see chapter 1 below.

7. This point is developed in David Potter's important essay "The

Historian's Use of Nationalism and Vice Versa" (1962), in his *The South and the Sectional Conflict* (Baton Rouge: Louisiana State University Press, 1968), 34–83.

8. William Gilmore Simms, quoted in John McCardell, *The Idea of a Southern Nation: Southern Nationalists and Southern Nationalism, 1830–1860* (New York: W. W. Norton, 1979), 143.

1. Federalism, Republicanism, and the Origins of American Sectionalism

Thanks to Ed Ayers, Mike Holt, Jan Lewis, and Kristin Onuf for critical comments.

1. On the construction of sectional histories and stereotypes in antebellum America see William R. Taylor, *Cavalier and Yankee: The Old South and the American National Character* (New York: George Braziller, 1961). See also John McCardell, *The Idea of a Southern Nation: Southern Nationalists and Southern Nationalism, 1830–1860* (New York: W. W. Norton, 1979). On the centrality of questions of character in early American political thought see Peter S. Onuf and Nicholas G. Onuf, *Federal Union, Modern World: The Law of Nations in an Age of Revolutions, 1776–1814* (Madison: Madison House, 1993), 21.

2. See the essays collected in Robert Forster and Jack P. Greene, eds., *Preconditions of Revolution in Early Modern Europe* (Baltimore: Johns Hopkins University Press, 1970).

3. The literature on American nationalism is extensive. Useful general treatments include Yehoshua Arieli, *Individualism and Nationalism in American Ideology* (Cambridge: Harvard University Press, 1964); Merle Curti, *The Roots of American Loyalty* (New York: Columbia University Press, 1946); Paul C. Nagel, *One Nation Indivisible: The Union in American Thought, 1776–1861* (New York: Oxford University Press, 1964); idem, *This Sacred Trust: American Nationality, 1798–1898* (New York: Oxford University Press, 1971); and Wilbur Zelinsky, *Nation into State: The Shifting Symbolic Foundations of American Nationalism* (Chapel Hill: University of North Carolina Press, 1988).

4. My understanding of early American political geography is indebted to Jack P. Greene, *Peripheries and Center: Constitutional Development in the Extended Polities of the British Empire and the United States, 1607–1788* (Athens: University of Georgia Press, 1986).

5. Rosemarie Zagarri, *The Politics of Size: Representation in the United*

States, 1776–1850 (Ithaca: Cornell University Press, 1987); Elisha P. Douglass, *Rebels and Democrats: The Struggle for Equal Political Rights and Majority Rule during the American Revolution* (Chapel Hill: University of North Carolina Press, 1955); J. R. Pole, *Political Representation in England and the Origins of the American Republic* (New York: St. Martin's, 1966).

6. On British imperial patriotism and American nationality see the provocative essay by John M. Murrin, "A Roof without Walls: The Dilemma of American National Identity," in *Beyond Confederation: Origins of the Constitution and American National Identity,* ed. Richard Beeman et al. (Chapel Hill: University of North Carolina Press, 1987), 333–48. However, I dissent from Murrin's conclusion that "American national identity was . . . an unexpected, impromptu, artificial, and therefore extremely fragile creation of the Revolution" (344). Linda Colley shows that the construction of a *British* national identity was itself a recent and continuing development at the time of the American Revolution (*Britons: Forging the Nation, 1707–1837* [New Haven: Yale University Press, 1992]). Liah Greenfeld argues that the idea of an English nation, if not the broadening popular consciousness delineated by Colley, emerged in the seventeenth century (*Nationalism: Five Roads to Modernity* [Cambridge: Harvard University Press, 1992], 27–87). The discrepancy between Colley and Greenfeld may result from Greenfeld's conflation of high political theory—and the status concerns of the narrowly defined class of great men who constituted the "political nation"—with popular political consciousness. This elision enables her to assert, misleadingly, that "the English settlers came [to America] with a national identity" (402), when the definition of *British* nationality was itself the centrally controversial issue in the resistance movement.

7. Edmund S. Morgan's *Inventing the People: The Rise of Popular Sovereignty in England and America* (New York: W. W. Norton, 1988) offers an illuminating conceptual history of this "fiction" but does not discuss its geopolitical implications.

8. On state capitals see Zagarri, *Politics of Size,* 8–35; on the national capital, Kenneth R. Bowling, *The Creation of Washington, D.C.: The Idea and Location of the American Capital* (Fairfax, Va.: George Mason University Press, 1991).

9. On the permeability of state boundaries see Joel Barlow, *Advice to the Privileged Orders, in the Several States of Europe* (New York, 1792), 76: for Americans, "whether the territory on which they live

were called New-York or Massachusetts is a matter of total indifference."

10. "It is the objective need for homogeneity [in industrial society] which is reflected in nationalism" (Ernest Gellner, *Nations and Nationalism* [Ithaca: Cornell University Press, 1983], 46).

11. The historic significance of American nationalism has become apparent as scholars have recognized that national identities are social constructions and that the relationship between nation and state is contingent. As long as the "old" nations of Europe were defined as natural, traditional, and culturally distinctive communities, the United States—the "first new nation"—would seem exceptional and anomalous. But the deconstruction and demystification of nationalism in recent scholarship has made American nationalism visible: if nationalism is artificial, the American Revolutionaries were its first great artificers. On the development of nationalism I am particularly indebted to Gellner, *Nations and Nationalism;* Benedict Anderson, *Imagined Communities: Reflections on the Origins and Spread of Nationalism,* rev. ed. (London: Verso, 1991); and E. J. Hobsbawm, *Nations and Nationalism since 1780,* 2nd ed. (Cambridge: Cambridge University Press, 1992). Tony Judt accuses Anderson and other scholars who emphasize the social construction of collective identities of not taking nationalism and national identity "seriously . . . on their own terms" ("The New Old Nationalism," *New York Review of Books,* 26 May 1994, 44–51, quotation on 45). Presumably Judt means that the inventiveness of nationalists is severely constrained by preexisting loyalties and identities and that, whatever their sources, national identities are deeply embedded in and inextricable from the experiences of peoples everywhere in the modern world. Nationalism should not be treated as "a historical mistake, a cognitive error to be made good by clear-sighted analytical demystification" (45).

12. Cathy D. Matson and Peter S. Onuf, *A Union of Interests: Political and Economic Thought in Revolutionary America* (Lawrence: University Press of Kansas, 1990), 83–86; "The Idea of Separate Confederacies," documents and editorial commentaries in *The Documentary History of the Ratification of the Constitution,* ed. John P. Kaminski et al., 11 vols. to date (Madison: State Historical Society of Wisconsin, 1976–), 13:54–59.

13. *The Federalist* (Middletown, Conn.: Wesleyan University Press, 1961), ed. Jacob E. Cooke, no. 7, 38, 39, 41.

14. James Madison, speech of 29 June, in Max Farrand, ed., *The Records of the Federal Convention of 1787*, 4 vols. (New Haven: Yale University Press, 1911–1937), 1:476 (Robert Yates's notes). See the discussions in Zagarri, *Politics of Size*, 76–78, and Matson and Onuf, *Union of Interests*, 110–13.

15. Peter S. Onuf, "Anarchy and the Crisis of the Union," in *To Form a More Perfect Union: The Critical Ideas of the Constitution*, ed. Herman Belz, Ronald Hoffman, and Peter J. Albert (Charlottesville: University Press of Virginia, 1992), 272–302.

16. Although Patrick Henry was accused of wanting to lead a new Southern confederation out of the union, there is no persuasive evidence that Antifederalists would have welcomed such an outcome. References to Henry's alleged support for separate unions are sprinkled throughout the Virginia volumes of the *Documentary History of the Ratification of the Constitution* (vols. 8–10). See, for example, Tobias Lear to John Langdon, 3 Dec. 1787, 8:197: "if I may be allowed to form an opinion, from his conduct, of what would be his wish, it is to divide the Southern States from the others. Should that take place, Virginia would hold the first place among them, & he the first place in Virginia." See also Edward Carrington to James Madison, 10 Feb. 1788, and Carrington to Thomas Jefferson, 24 Apr. 1788, 8:359 and 9:755. My sense is that it was not Antifederalists but future Federalists who, as they became increasingly desperate about the union's survival in the months leading up to the Philadelphia Convention, were more likely to consider the possibility of regional unions (Onuf, "Constitutional Politics: States, Sections, and the National Interest," in *Toward a More Perfect Union: Six Essays on the Constitution*, ed. Neil L. York [Provo, Utah: Brigham Young University Press, 1988], 40–43).

17. Item in *Independent Gazetteer* (Philadelphia), 22 Jan. 1788, in Kaminski et al., *Documentary History*, 2:657. For a good introduction to Antifederalist thought see Herbert J. Storing, *What the Anti-Federalists Were For*, vol. 1 of *The Complete Anti-Federalist*, 7 vols., ed. Storing (Chicago: University of Chicago Press, 1981).

18. "The Dissent of the Minority," *Pennsylvania Packet*, 18 Dec. 1787, in Kaminski et al., *Documentary History*, 2:626.

19. [Melancton Smith?], "Letters from the Federal Farmer," no. 2, 9 Oct. 1787, reprinted in Paul Leicester Ford, ed., *Pamphlets on the Constitution of the United States* (Brooklyn, 1888), 290.

20. [John Winthrop], "Agrippa," no. 13, 14 Jan. 1788, in Paul

Leicester Ford, ed., *Essays on the Constitution of the United States* (Brooklyn, 1892), 98.

21. Antifederalists could not not agree on *which* existing region would benefit the most, and Federalists quickly recognized and exploited these contradictory predictions. See Madison's survey of opposition to ratification across the continent in a letter to Edmund Randolph, 10 Jan. 1788, in Kaminski et al., *Documentary History*, 8:288–91.

22. Fears of a dominant metropolis were expressed most explicitly in Antifederalist commentary on the proposed federal district. "This ten miles square," George Mason asserted, "may set at defiance the laws of the surrounding States, and may . . . become the sanctuary of the blackest crimes" (speech of 16 June 1788, Virginia Convention, in Kaminski et al., *Documentary History*, 10:1317). For a discussion of the site issue in the ratification debates see Bowling, *Creation of Washington, D.C.*, 74–105; see also James Sterling Young, *The Washington Community, 1800–1828* (New York: Columbia University Press, 1966), chap. 1.

23. The ratification controversy is conveniently discussed on a state-by-state basis in Michael Gillespie and Michael Lienesch, eds., *Ratifying the Constitution* (Lawrence: University Press of Kansas, 1989).

24. Michael Kammen, *Empire and Interest: The American Colonies and the Politics of Mercantilism* (Philadelphia: Lippincott, 1970), 116–37.

25. Frederick W. Marks III, *Independence on Trial: Foreign Affairs and the Making of the Constitution* (Baton Rouge: Louisiana State University Press, 1973).

26. H. Jefferson Powell, "The Original Understanding of Original Intent," *Harvard Law Review* 98 (1985), 885–948.

27. *The Federalist*, no. 37, 236–37.

28. Gordon S. Wood, "Conspiracy and the Paranoid Style: Causality and Deceit in the Eighteenth Century," *William and Mary Quarterly*, 3rd ser., 39 (1982), 401–41.

29. On the Antifederalists' transformation into strict constructionist defenders of the new Constitution see Lance Banning, "Republican Ideology and the Triumph of the Constitution, 1789–1793," *William and Mary Quarterly* 31 (1974), 167–88; and Richard E. Ellis, "The Persistence of Antifederalism after 1789," in Beeman et al., *Beyond Confederation*, 295–314.

30. Paul Finkelman, "Slavery and the Constitutional Convention:

Making a Covenant with Death," in Beeman et al., *Beyond Confederation*, 188–225.

31. Peter S. Onuf, "Articles of Confederation," in *The Framing and Ratification of the Constitution*, ed. Leonard Levy and Dennis Mahoney (New York: Macmillan, 1986), 82–97; Jack N. Rakove, "From One Agenda to Another: The Condition of American Federalism, 1783–1787," in *The American Revolution: Its Character and Limits*, ed. Jack P. Greene (New York: New York University Press, 1987), 80–103.

32. Edmund Randolph, speeches, 1 and 2 June; Gouverneur Morris, speech and proceedings, 29 Aug. 1787, in Farrand, *Records of the Federal Convention*, 1:66, 88; 2:454–55.

33. For further discussion and citations see Peter S. Onuf, *The Origins of the Federal Republic: Jurisdictional Controversies in the United States, 1775–1787* (Philadelphia: University of Pennsylvania Press, 1983), 207–9.

34. See, for example, Patrick Henry's warning that the new regime would enable the Northern states to "give away" the navigation of the Mississippi: "The southern parts of America have been protected by that weakness [of the Articles] so much execrated" (speech of 9 June 1788, Virginia Convention, in Kaminski et al., *Documentary History*, 9:1051).

35. According to Joyce Appleby, "Virginia nationalists . . . dominated American politics after 1783 and led the campaign to establish a 'more perfect union' four years later"; Jeffersonians subsequently drew support from an emergent wheat-growing region extending from Virginia to New York, which superseded "conventional divisions of North and South" ("The 'Agrarian Myth' in the Early Republic," in Appleby, *Liberalism and Republicanism in the Historical Imagination* [Cambridge: Harvard University Press, 1992], 272, 268). For suggestive comments on the transition to wheat and the importance of Western lands to Revolutionary Virginians see T. H. Breen, *Tobacco Culture: The Mentality of the Great Tidewater Planters on the Eve of Revolution* (Princeton: Princeton University Press, 1985), 180–86, 204–10. On Virginia expansionism see Marc Egnal, "The Origins of the Revolution in Virginia: A Reinterpretation," *William and Mary Quarterly* 37 (1980), 401–28; and idem, *A Mighty Empire: The Origins of the American Revolution* (Ithaca: Cornell University Press, 1988).

36. For the development of these sectional alliances see H. James Henderson, "The Structure of Politics in the Continental Congress,"

in *Essays on the American Revolution*, ed. Stephen G. Kurtz and James H. Hutson (Chapel Hill: University of North Carolina Press, 1973), 157–96; Henderson, *Party Politics in the Continental Congress* (New York: McGraw-Hill, 1974); and Joseph L. Davis, *Sectionalism in American Politics, 1774–1787* (Madison: University of Wisconsin Press, 1977).

37. Drew R. McCoy, "James Madison and Visions of American Nationality in the Confederation Period: A Regional Perspective," in Beeman et al., *Beyond Confederation*, 226–58; Lance Banning, "Virginia: Sectionalism, and the General Good," in Gillespie and Lienesch, *Ratifying the Constitution*, 261–99. On Virginia's position "'at the centre of the states'" see Jack P. Greene, "The Constitution of 1787 and the Question of Southern Distinctiveness," in Greene, *Imperatives, Behaviors, and Identities: Essays in Early American Cultural History* (Charlottesville: University Press of Virginia, 1992), 327–47, esp. 340–43, quotation on 342.

38. My discussion here is indebted to Jack P. Greene, "The Intellectual Reconstruction of Virginia," in *Jeffersonian Legacies*, ed. Peter S. Onuf (Charlottesville: University Press of Virginia, 1993), 225–53.

39. Ibid., 242–45. Paul Finkelman demonstrates the discrepancy between such professions and actual practice in "Jefferson and Slavery: 'Treason against the Hopes of the World,' " in Onuf, *Jeffersonian Legacies*, 181–221. On the entrenchment of the institution in Virginia during this period see Robert McColley, *Slavery in Jeffersonian Virginia*, 2nd ed. (Urbana: University of Illinois Press, 1972).

40. John Daly Burk, *History of Virginia*, 4 vols. (Richmond, 1804–16), 1:212, as cited by Greene in "Intellectual Reconstruction of Virginia," 244.

41. On the widespread support for "conditional termination" see William W. Freehling, *The Road to Disunion: Secessionists at Bay, 1776–1854* (New York: Oxford University Press), 121–43.

42. William Lloyd Garrison, editorial, *The Liberator*, 17 Mar. 1843, quoted in Aileen S. Kraditor, *Means and Ends in American Abolitionism: Garrison and His Critics on Strategy and Tactics, 1834–1850* (New York: Pantheon Books, 1969), 200.

43. Onuf, *Origins of the Federal Republic*, 158–60.

44. *Boston Independent Chronicle*, 15 Feb. 1787, in Kaminski et al., *Documentary History*, 13:57. For a discussion of the distinctiveness of New England's colonial history see Jack P. Greene, *Pursuits of Happi-*

ness: The Social Development of Early Modern British Colonies and the Formation of American Culture (Chapel Hill: University of North Carolina Press, 1988), 55–80.

45. [James Madison], "Consolidation," *National Gazette*, 5 Dec. 1791, in *The Papers of James Madison, Congressional Series*, ed. J. C. A. Stagg et al., 17 vols. (Chicago and Charlottesville: University of Chicago Press and University Press of Virginia, 1962–91), 14:138.

46. "The Politician," New York, 21 Oct. 1790, in *American Museum* 7 (1790), 145.

47. James Hall, *Letters from the West* (1828; Gainesville, Fla.: Scholars' Facsimiles, 1967), letter 15, "National Character," 246. For analysis of travelers' accounts, a good source for sectional stereotypes, see John Jakle, *Images of the Ohio Valley: A Historical Geography of Travel, 1740 to 1860* (New York: Oxford University Press, 1977).

48. Peter S. Onuf, *Statehood and Union: A History of the Northwest Ordinance* (Bloomington: Indiana University Press, 1987), 146–52. Frederick Jackson Turner's "frontier thesis" was the ultimate expression of Midwestern patriotism and was premised on the conflation of regional and national identities (Andrew R. L. Cayton and Peter S. Onuf, *The Midwest and the Nation: Rethinking the History of an American Region* [Bloomington: Indiana University Press, 1990], xv–xvii, 125–26).

49. James Jackson, speech to the Senate, 25 Feb. 1803, *Annals of the Congress of the United States, 1789–1824*, 42 vols. (Washington, D.C., 1834–56), 7th Cong., 2nd sess., 243.

50. Peter S. Onuf, "The Expanding Union," in *Devising Liberty: The Conditions of Freedom in the Early American Republic*, ed. David T. Konig (Stanford: Stanford University Press, 1995), 50–80, 312–20; Arthur P. Whitaker, *The Mississippi Question, 1795–1803* (New York: Appleton-Century, 1934), 189–236.

51. The definitive account is Thomas Perkins Abernethy, *The Burr Conspiracy* (New York: Oxford University Press, 1954).

52. Malcolm Rohrbough, *The Land Office Business: The Settlement and Administration of American Public Lands, 1789–1837* (New York: Oxford University Press, 1968); Daniel Feller, *The Public Lands in Jacksonian Politics* (Madison: University of Wisconsin Press, 1984).

53. Harry N. Scheiber, *Ohio Canal Era: A Case Study of Government and the Economy, 1820–1861* (Athens: Ohio University Press, 1968).

54. My analysis is indebted to John Lauritz Larson, " 'Bind the

Republic Together': The National Union and the Struggle for a System of Internal Improvements," *Journal of American History* 74 (1987), 363–87. See also George Rogers Taylor, *The Transportation Revolution, 1815–1860* (New York: Rinehart, 1951).

55. For good treatments of Clay's thought see Peter B. Knupfer, *The Union As It Is: Constitutional Unionism and Sectional Compromise, 1787–1861* (Chapel Hill: University of North Carolina Press, 1991), 119–57; and James E. Lewis, " 'We Shall Have Good Neighbours': The American Union and the Collapse of the Spanish Empire, 1783–1829" (Ph.D. diss., University of Virginia, 1994), chap. 4.

56. For a suggestive discussion of the relation between republicanism and nationalism in the context of party polarization see Jean H. Baker, *Affairs of Party: The Political Culture of Northern Democrats in the Mid-Nineteenth Century* (Ithaca: Cornell University Press, 1983), 143–211.

57. Lance Banning, *The Jeffersonian Persuasion: Evolution of a Party Ideology* (Ithaca: Cornell University Press, 1978), 246–302; Richard Hofstadter, *The Idea of a Party System: The Rise of Legitimate Opposition in the United States, 1780–1840* (Berkeley and Los Angeles: University of California Press, 1970), 122–69. Although Jefferson believed that "the body of our countrymen is substantially republican through every part of the Union," he was also convinced "that we are compleatly under the saddle of Massachusets & Connecticut" and their "eastern" allies (Jefferson to John Taylor, 4 June 1798. On the dangerous prevalence of monarchical and consolidationist principles in the New England states see Jefferson to Gideon Granger, 13 Aug. 1800, in Thomas Jefferson, *Writings*, ed. Merrill D. Peterson [New York: Library of America, 1984], 1049, 1079).

58. The most comprehensive treatment of this period is Stanley Elkins and Eric McKitrick, *The Age of Federalism* (New York: Oxford University Press, 1993). But for a discussion of the importance of sectionalism for party conflict see James Roger Sharp, *American Politics in the Early Republic: The New Nation in Crisis* (New Haven: Yale University Press, 1993). For an excellent treatment of Jeffersonian constitutionalism see David N. Mayer, *The Constitutional Thought of Thomas Jefferson* (Charlottesville: University Press of Virginia, 1994), esp. 119–221 (on federalism).

59. First Inaugural Address, 4 Mar. 1801, in Jefferson, *Writings*, 493–94. Peterson capitalizes *Republicans* and *Federalists*, though, as he

notes (1555), they are not capitalized in the manuscript or in many print versions. It is clear that the "federal principles" referred to here are not those of the Federalist party.

60. Joyce Appleby best captures this progressive dimension of the Jeffersonian appeal in *Capitalism and a New Social Order: The Republican Vision of the 1790s* (New York: New York University Press, 1984). For further discussion and citations see Peter S. Onuf, "The Scholars' Jefferson," *William and Mary Quarterly* 50 (1993), 671–99.

61. Here I rely heavily on Knupfer, *The Union As It Is*.

62. Jefferson to John Holmes, 22 Apr. 1820, in Jefferson, *Writings*, 1434. The most comprehensive study remains Glover Moore, *The Missouri Controversy, 1819–1821* (Lexington: University of Kentucky Press, 1953). See also Freehling, *Road to Disunion*, 144–61.

63. See Drew R. McCoy's insightful treatment of this theme in *The Last of the Fathers: James Madison and the Republican Legacy* (New York: Cambridge University Press, 1989), 119–70.

64. On the second crisis of the union and its impact on Adams and Clay I am indebted to Lewis, "We Shall Have Good Neighbours," chaps. 2–4. On Jackson see Richard E. Ellis, *The Union at Risk: Jacksonian Democracy, States' Rights, and the Nullification Crisis* (New York: Oxford University Press, 1987).

65. It was the founders' "task (and nobly they performed it) to possess themselves . . . of this goodly land; and to uprear upon its hills and its valleys, a political edifice of liberty and equal rights; 'tis ours only, to transmit these . . . to the latest generation" (Lincoln, Address before the Young Men's Lyceum of Springfield, Illinois, 27 Jan. 1838, in *The Collected Works of Abraham Lincoln*, ed. Roy P. Basler, 9 vols. [New Brunswick: Rutgers University Press, 1953], 1:108. See the discussion in George Forgie, *Patricide in the House Divided: A Psychological Interpretation of Lincoln and His Age* [New York: W. W. Norton, 1979]).

66. For a full elaboration of this perspective see John Taylor, *Tyranny Unmasked*, ed. F. Thornton Miller (1821; reprint, Indianapolis: Liberty Classics, 1992). See also Jesse T. Carpenter, *The South as a Conscious Minority* (New York: New York University Press, 1930).

67. The best treatment of the antipower theme remains Bernard Bailyn, *The Ideological Origins of the American Revolution* (Cambridge: Harvard University Press, 1967), 55–93.

68. William J. Cooper, *The South and the Politics of Slavery, 1828–1856* (Baton Rouge: Louisiana State University Press, 1978), demon-

strates the limits of Southerners' commitments to national parties and
their rising demands for concessions from coadjutors in other sections.
For a brilliant analysis of the ways in which party competition could
"contain" "sectional conflict" see Michael F. Holt, *The Political Crisis of
the 1850s* (New York: John Wiley, 1978). But "once faith in those parties
collapsed . . . , a sense of crisis developed that government was
beyond control of the people, that it had become a threatening power
dominated by some gigantic conspiracy, and hence that republican institutions were under attack" (258). For a thorough treatment of republican anxieties and appeals in one state see J. Mills Thornton III,
Politics and Power in a Slave Society: Alabama, 1800–1860 (Baton Rouge:
Louisiana State University Press, 1978), 343–461.

2. New England as Region and Nation

Epigraph: I presented an earlier version of this essay, under the title
"Inventing New England," at the University of Mississippi's Chancellor
M. Porter Symposium "The New Regionalism" in October 1993. I am
grateful to Charles R. Wilson of the University of Mississippi and to the
University of Mississippi Press, which published the proceedings of that
symposium, for graciously allowing me to use much of that material
here. In addition, parts of this essay are about other people's work, and
it gives me pleasure to thank here several friends for planting ideas that
have stayed with me and that deeply inform my own work (additional
debts are acknowledged in the text proper): Gary Kulik started me
thinking about these issues, and coined a version of my earlier title,
"The Invention of New England." Joseph Conforti's work with the
New England Studies program at the University of Southern Maine
has kept me thinking about the subject and has been over these past
six years a continual source of new questions and materials, including
several that are crucial to my argument here. Robert A. Gross and Michael Winship have each shared splendid thoughts out of an ample
store. Finally, Dona Brown and I have spoken so often with each other
about the politics of New England culture that I cannot know how to
know where my debt to her ends or begins.

1. See also, for example, D. W. Griffith's 1921 film set in Maine,
Way Down East, in which the rural characters look, act, and speak like
figures out of the "Dogpatch" comic strip.

2. Thornton Wilder, *Our Town* (New York, 1938), 10. To create "our

town," the presence of French-Canadians in northern New England needs to be actively forgotten. Indeed, they remain the least-studied and -noticed group in New England. Such immigrant New Englanders will not directly appear in this essay either. Still, their presence informs it. I myself have studied mostly the middle and upper classes, the historical as well as the literary "canon," as it were. But I have studied them through the reflecting mirror of what other scholars have unearthed about the lives of laboring people, women, and minorities. In short, I have devoted much of my scholarly attention, and I devote much of this essay as well, to a reevaluation of the hegemonic culture in the light of what we now know about the counterculture.

3. For the cultural relationship between Old and New England see David D. Hall, *Worlds of Wonder, Days of Judgment: Popular Religious Belief in Early New England* (New York: Knopf, 1989); and Richard Godbeer, *The Devil's Dominion: Magic and Religion in Early New England* (Cambridge: Cambridge University Press, 1992).

4. See, for example, Stephen Innes, *Labor in a New Land: Economy and Society in Seventeenth-Century Springfield* (Princeton: Princeton University Press, 1983); Christine Leigh Heyrman, *Commerce and Culture: The Maritime Communities of Colonial Massachusetts, 1690–1750* (New York: W. W. Norton, 1984); John F. Martin, *Profits in the Wilderness: Entrepreneurship and the Founding of New England Towns in the Seventeenth Century* (Chapel Hill: University of North Carolina Press, 1991); and Karen Ordahl Kupperman, *Providence Island, 1630–1641: The Other Puritan Colony* (Cambridge: Cambridge University Press, 1993).

5. Martyn J. Bowden, "Culture and Place: English Sub-Cultural Regions in New England in the Seventeenth Century," *Connecticut History* 35 (1994), 68–146.

6. Harriet Beecher Stowe, *The Pearl of Orr's Island: A Story of the Coast of Maine* (Boston, 1862), chap. 3; "rude and primitive singing" is from Stowe, *Oldtown Folks* (Boston, 1869), chap. 5.

7. The group is the Bailey-Hazen Singers, formerly the Word of Mouth Chorus. Let me quote from the dust jacket of their record album *Rivers of Delight* (Nonesuch H-71360): "Founded in 1972, the Word of Mouth Chorus is based in Plainfield, Vermont, and is active throughout New England. . . . Many of us first sang Sacred Harp music together in 1971. . . . In April 1976, a group of Word of Mouth Singers traveled to the Georgia State Singing Convention and were profoundly impressed by this . . . experience with the ongoing Southern shape-

note tradition. . . . Moreover, the singing itself—the rhythmic drive, the unrestrained quality of the voices, the sheer power of the sound— permanently altered our approach to Sacred Harp music."

8. Martyn Bowden, untitled typescript, 1993, 1.

9. Charles Dickens, *American Notes for General Circulation* (New York, 1842), 75.

10. Christopher Clark, *The Roots of Rural Capitalism: Western Massachusetts, 1780–1860* (Ithaca: Cornell University Press, 1990). See also Joseph Wood, "Village and Community in Early Colonial New England," *Journal of Historical Geography* 8 (1982), 333–46; and idem, " 'Build, Therefore, Your Own World': The New England Village as Settlement Ideal," *Annals of the Association of American Geographers* 80 (1991), 32–50.

11. William Butler, "Another City upon a Hill: Litchfield, Connecticut, and the Colonial Revival," in *The Colonial Revival in America*, ed. Alan Axelrod (New York: W. W. Norton, 1985), 15–51. See also Martyn J. Bowden, "The Invention of American Tradition," *Journal of Historical Geography* 18 (1992), 3–26; and Joseph S. Wood, "A World We Have Gained: House, Common, and Village in New England," ibid., 105–20.

12. Timothy Dwight, *Travels in New England and New York*, ed. Barbara Miller Solomon, 4 vols. (Cambridge: Harvard University Press, 1969).

13. Peter Onuf has shown that secessionist ideas in New England go back to the 1780s (see chapter 1).

14. Dwight, *Travels in New England and New York*, 1:244–46. Dwight noted at another point: "We have in New England no such class of men as . . . are denominated peasantry" (4:244).

15. William R. Taylor has shown how the New England "Yankee" and the Southern "Cavalier" were devised at the same moment, and in direct relation to each other, in his *Cavalier and Yankee: The Old South and the American National Character* (New York: George Braziller, 1961). This book remains a model and an inspiration three decades after publication.

16. John Winthrop, "A Model of Christian Charity," ed. Stephen Nissenbaum, in *The Course of United States History*, ed. David Nasaw, 2 vols. (Chicago: Dorsey, 1987), 1:51.

17. Daniel Webster, *The Writings and Speeches of Daniel Webster*, 18 vols. (Boston, 1903), 4:222–23.

18. For another version of the relationship between industrialization, evangelical Christianity, westward expansion, and the New England village ideal, see Daniel Walker Howe, *The Political Culture of the American Whigs* (Chicago: University of Chicago Press, 1979), 96–105, 150–67. Howe too suggests that during the 1830s "economic innovation and social stability could still seem compatible" (105).

19. The best account of the relationship between industrialization and nineteenth-century New England rural life is Hal Barron, *Those Who Stayed Behind: Rural Society in Nineteenth-Century New England* (New York: Cambridge University Press, 1984).

20. Lyman Beecher Stowe, *Saints, Sinners, and Beechers* (Indianapolis: Bobbs-Merrill, 1934), 55, quoted in Robert H. Abzug, *Passionate Liberator: Theodore Dwight Weld and the Dilemma of Reform* (New York: Oxford University Press, 1980), 76.

21. Lyman Beecher, *A Plea for the West* (Cincinnati, 1835), 36–37, quoted in Abzug, *Passionate Liberator*, 78.

22. Ralph Waldo Emerson, "Self-Reliance," in *Essays, First Series*, in *The Complete Works of Ralph Waldo Emerson*, Centenary Edition, 12 vols. (Boston, 1903–4), 2:53.

23. For Lyman Beecher's position on slavery, see *The Autobiography of Lyman Beecher*, ed. Barbara M. Cross, 2 vols. (Cambridge: Harvard University Press, 1961), 2:242. The Lane revolt is described on pp. 240–49 and in many other places.

24. Harriet Beecher Stowe, *Uncle Tom's Cabin: or, Life among the Lowly* (New York: New American Library, Signet Classic, 1981). The slaves even engage in singing hymns with a "nasal intonation" (77), another link to Stowe's childhood in Litchfield.

25. Ibid., 232, 247, 290.

26. Dona Brown, "Vacationing in Sarah Orne Jewett's *Deephaven*" (paper delivered at conference, "Borrowing Enchantment: Sarah Jewett's Invention of Rural Maine," South Berwick, Maine, 26 June 1994); Richard H. Brodhead, *Culture of Letters: Scenes of Reading and Writing in Nineteenth-Century America* (Chicago: University of Chicago Press, 1993), esp. 115–76.

27. Joel Garreau, *The Nine Nations of North America* (Boston: Houghton Mifflin, 1984), 15–48, esp. 17–18.

28. For an analysis of this subject see Eric Sager and Gerald Panting, *Maritime Capital: The Shipping Industry in Atlantic Canada, 1820–1914*

(Montreal: McGill-Queens University Press, 1990). I am indebted to David Beattie of Mt. Allison University, Sackville, New Brunswick, who referred me to this book. See also Kris Inwood, ed., *Farm, Factory, and Fortune: New Studies in the Economic History of the Maritime Provinces* (Fredericton, New Brunswick: Acadiensis, 1993); and T. W. Acheson, *Industrialization and Underdevelopment in the Maritimes, 1880–1920* (Toronto: Garamond, 1985). I was alerted to these two titles by David Jaffee.

3. What We Talk about When We Talk about the South

1. Benjamin N. Smith, "Southern Discomfort," *Harvard Crimson*, 6 Apr. 1985, 2. Molly Hatchett was one of the many rock groups who rode a Southern Rock wave in the 1970s and 1980s, reveling in Southern accents, country and blues styles, and Confederate flags.

2. Peter Gould and Rodney White, *Mental Maps*, 2nd ed. (Boston: Allen & Unwin, 1986), 53–72.

3. See the findings reported in the influential series of books by John Shelton Reed: *The Enduring South: Subcultural Persistence in Mass Society* (Lexington, Mass.: D. C. Heath, 1972); *One South: An Ethnic Approach to Regional Culture* (Baton Rouge: Louisiana State University Press, 1982); *Southerners: The Social Psychology of Sectionalism* (Chapel Hill: University of North Carolina Press, 1983).

4. Eddy L. Harris, *South of Haunted Dreams: A Ride through Slavery's Old Back Yard* (New York: Simon & Schuster, 1993), 232–33; Ray Allen, "Back Home: Southern Identity and African-American Gospel Quartet Performance," in *Mapping American Culture*, ed. Wayne Franklin and Michael Steiner (Iowa City: University of Iowa Press, 1992), 112–35. This is not the first generation to wrestle with such issues; see Arna Bontemps, "Why I Returned," in *Voices in Black and White: Writings on Race in America from Harper's Magazine*, ed. Henry Louis Gates Jr. (New York: Franklin Square, 1993), 33–45; and Ralph Ellison, *Going to the Territory* (New York: Vintage Books, 1987). As Ellison wrote, "In relation to their Southern background, the cultural history of Negroes in the North reads like the legend of some tragic people out of mythology, a people which aspired to escape from its own unhappy homeland to the apparent peace of a distant mountain; but, in migrat-

ing, made some fatal error of judgment and fell into a great chasm of mazelike passages that promise ever to lead to the mountain but end ever against a wall" (298–99; also see 89–103).

5. *New York Times*, 31 July 1994, A1; Harris, *South of Haunted Dreams*, 152.

6. "Tennessee," on the compact disc *Three Years Five Months and Two Days in the Life of . . .* , by Arrested Development (EMI, 1992), deals eloquently with these issues; for a revealing interview with the lyricist for Arrested Development see Bill Flanagan, "Black History: Speech Meets Curtis Mayfield," *Musician*, June 1993, 60–67.

7. The pioneering work in this field is David Potter's seminal essay "The Historian's Use of Nationalism and Vice Versa," in *The South and the Sectional Conflict* (Baton Rouge: Louisiana State University Press, 1968), 34–83. For Potter's strictures on Southern difference see 181–82.

8. For a useful statement of such ideas that fuses anthropology and geography, see Arjun Appadurai, "Putting Hierarchy in Its Place," *Cultural Anthropology* 3 (1988), 36–49. I first encountered the incentive to rethink "natural" boundaries in Richard Handler's *Nationalism and the Politics of Culture in Quebec* (Madison: University of Wisconsin, 1988). Of more immediate relevance but also more problematic because of its reductionist focus on a world system is Immanuel Wallerstein, "What Can One Mean by Southern Culture?" in *The Evolution of Southern Culture*, ed. Numan Bartley (Athens: University of Georgia Press, 1988), 1–13. For other relevant and related ideas see Benedict Anderson, *Imagined Communities: Reflections on the Origins and Spread of Nationalism*, rev. ed. (London: Verso, 1991); Linda Colley, *Britons: Forging the Nation, 1707–1837* (New Haven: Yale University Press, 1992); Liah Greenfeld, *Nationalism: Five Roads to Modernity* (Cambridge: Harvard University Press, 1992); Jack Temple Kirby, *Media-Made Dixie: The South in the American Imagination* (Baton Rouge: Louisiana State University Press, 1978); Werner Sollors, *Beyond Ethnicity: Consent and Descent in American Culture* (New York: Oxford University Press, 1986); James C. Cobb, "Tomorrow Seems Like Yesterday: The South's Future in the Nation and the World," in *The Future South: A Historical Perspective for the Twenty-first Century*, ed. Joe P. Dunn and Howard L. Preston (Urbana: University of Illinois Press, 1991), 217–38.

My own first book, *Vengeance and Justice: Crime and Punishment in the Nineteenth-Century American South* (New York: Oxford University

Press, 1984), seems in retrospect to have been a strong offender in creating the South as "The Other," sharply bifurcating Northern from Southern culture. While I still believe in the way I described Southern honor, I would not now paint things in such dichotomous ways.

9. The city fathers of the hard-luck mining town of Appalachia, Virginia, for example, are trying to capitalize on the fortuitous name of their town to create a useful fiction: "If we can create the myth of Appalachia being the past center of mountain life," the city manager explains, "then we can reap the benefits from the only thing we have to sell, the name Appalachia." Even as the real coal mines shut down and young people leave for elsewhere, the town plans to open an exhibition mine and offer certification attesting to visitors' identity as honorary Appalachians (Jeannie Ralston, "In the Heart of Appalachia," *National Geographic,* Feb. 1993, 132).

10. The influential text in this regard is Eric Hobsbawm and Terence Ranger, eds., *The Invention of Tradition* (New York: Cambridge University Press, 1983).

11. Doris Betts first presented such a list in "Many Souths and Broadening Scale: A Changing Southern Literature," in Dunn and Preston, *The Future South,* 177–78.

12. John Egerton, *Shades of Gray: Dispatches from the Modern South* (Baton Rouge: Louisiana State University Press, 1991), 255–60.

13. James W. Fernandez, "Andalusia on Our Minds: Two Contrasting Places in Spain As Seen in a Vernacular Poetic Duel of the Late Nineteenth Century," *Cultural Anthropology* 3 (1988), 21–35. Other interesting works in the "new geography" or "new regionalism" include: Appadurai, "Putting Hierarchy in Its Place"; J. Nicholas Entrikin, *The Betweenness of Place: Towards a Geography of Modernity* (Baltimore: Johns Hopkins University Press, 1991); Akhil Gupta and James Ferguson, "Beyond 'Culture': Space, Identity, and the Politics of Difference," *Cultural Anthropology* 7 (Feb. 1992), 6–23; Liisa Malkki, "National Geographic: The Rooting of Peoples and the Territorialization of National Identity among Refugees and Scholars," ibid., 24–44. Especially useful is Allan Pred, *Making Histories and Constructing Human Geographies: The Local Transformation of Practice, Power Relations, and Consciousness* (Boulder: Westview, 1990). Thomas Jefferson summarized these characteristics in a famous letter to the Marquis de Chastellux, quoted in Gary Wills's *Inventing America: Jefferson's Declaration of Independence* (New York: Vintage Books, 1978), 283–84.

A 1993 survey of over three hundred undergraduates at the University of Virginia—young people from thirty-three different states, of diverse ethnicities, fewer than half of whom consider themselves Southerners—showed that the perception of Southern distinctiveness is alive and well. Of those who considered themselves Southerners, black and white, almost all declared themselves proud of that identity, with women and African Americans being the most likely to take pride in their regional background.

What sets the South apart in these young people's eyes? When they were asked to rank twenty-eight different attributes on a scale of Southernness, several traits consistently appeared at the top of the list. Speech, not surprisingly, struck almost everyone as different in the South. But beyond that, people commented most on the South's courtesy, hospitality, sense of history, and natural beauty. Black and white students had similar notions of what set the South apart except on one issue: African Americans ranked racism fourth, while white students ranked it tenth. These are very similar to the patterns found in the polls analyzed by John Shelton Reed in *Enduring South*.

Just about everyone I have casually queried, regardless of any regionality they may claim, agrees with this characterization of Southerners, black and white, as "nice." It seems to be perhaps the most tangible evidence of a Southern upbringing. Why? I think it may originally have been related to the fact that white people and black people were forced to live together despite reasons for hatred on one side and fear on the other. Now, it seems to be pursued for its own sake, a style that envelops and to some extent obscures other differences and conflicts. It can be put to the use of virtually any purpose, modern or antimodern.

14. William R. Taylor, *Cavalier and Yankee: The Old South and the American National Character* (New York: George Braziller, 1961).

15. Sollors, *Beyond Ethnicity*, 190.

16. Michael Montgomery, "The Southern Accent—Alive and Well," *Southern Cultures* 1 (1993), 47–64.

17. Richard Graham, "Economics or Culture? The Development of the U.S. South and Brazil in the Days of Slavery," in *What Made the South Different?* ed. Kees Gispen (Oxford: University of Mississippi Press, 1990).

18. For a contrasting argument, see A. Cash Koeniger, "Climate and

Southern Distinctiveness," *Journal of Southern History* 54 (1988), 21–44.

19. For pioneering and exciting work in this vein, see Michael O'Brien, *Rethinking the South: Essays in Intellectual History* (Baltimore: Johns Hopkins University Press, 1988), 38–56. O'Brien's other work on Southern intellectual history develops these perspectives in extremely useful ways: see *The Idea of the American South, 1920–1941* (Baltimore: Johns Hopkins University Press, 1979) and *All Clever Men, Who Make Their Way: Critical Discourse in the Old South* (Fayetteville: University of Arkansas Press, 1982).

20. See Drew Gilpin Faust, *The Creation of Confederate Nationalism: Ideology and Identity in the Civil War South* (Baton Rouge: Louisiana State University Press, 1988).

21. Faust, *Confederate Nationalism*, 10–11.

22. Colley, *Britons*, 5–6; Greenfeld, *Nationalism*, 476–77.

23. This point, among many others about the war, was made powerfully by Robert Penn Warren in his meditation *The Legacy of the Civil War* (New York: Random House, 1961).

24. Tracy Thompson, "The War between the States of Mind," *Washington Post*, 10 Jan. 1993.

25. William Faulkner, *The Faulkner Reader* (New York: Random House, 1954), 315. I would like to thank Brad Mittendorf for calling this quote to my attention.

26. Pred, *Making Histories*.

27. Louis D. Rubin Jr., *A Gallery of Southerners* (Baton Rouge: Louisiana State University Press, 1982), 206, 222.

4. Region and Reason

1. See Patricia Nelson Limerick, *The Legacy of Conquest: The Unbroken Past of the American West* (New York: W. W. Norton, 1987); and Patricia Nelson Limerick, Clyde A. Milner II, and Charles E. Rankin, *Trails: Toward a New Western History* (Lawrence: University Press of Kansas, 1991).

2. For the best examples of this approach at work, see the following by Richard White: *Land Use, Environment, and Social Change: The Shaping of Island County, Washington* (Seattle: University of Washington Press, 1980); *The Roots of Dependency: Subsistence, Environment, and So-*

cial Change (Lincoln: University of Nebraska Press, 1983); and *"It's Your Misfortune and None of My Own": A New History of the American West* (Norman: University of Oklahoma Press, 1991).

3. Limerick, *The Legacy of Conquest*, 349.

4. Many of these figures are discussed in Robert L. Dorman, *Revolt of the Provinces: The Regionalist Movement in America, 1920–1945* (Chapel Hill: University of North Carolina Press, 1993). See esp. Howard W. Odum and Harry Estill Moore, *American Regionalism: A Cultural-Historical Approach to National Integration* (New York: Henry Holt, 1938).

5. For a considerably more sophisticated analysis of antimodernism than the caricature I present here, see T. J. Jackson Lears, *No Place of Grace: Antimodernism and the Transformation of Culture* (New York: Pantheon Books, 1981).

6. Frederick Jackson Turner, *The Significance of the Frontier in American History* (New York: Frederick Ungar, 1963); Ray Allen Billington and Martin Ridge, *Westward Expansion: A History of the American Frontier* (New York: Macmillan, 1982).

7. Arthur Schlesinger Jr., *The Disuniting of America: Reflections on a Multicultural Society* (New York: Whittle, 1991).

8. See Patricia Nelson Limerick, "The Case of the Premature Departure: The Trans-Mississippi West and American History Textbooks," *Journal of American History* 78 (1992), 1380–94.

9. Donald Worster, in "Appraisal of *Legacy of Conquest*," *Western Historical Quarterly* 20 (1989), 304.

10. Walter Prescott Webb, *The Great Plains* (Lincoln: University of Nebraska Press, 1931); Wallace Stegner, *Beyond the Hundredth Meridian: John Wesley Powell and the Second Opening of the West* (Boston: Houghton Mifflin, 1953); Marc Reisner, *Cadillac Desert: The American West and Its Disappearing Water* (New York: Viking, 1986); Donald Worster, *Rivers of Empire: Water, Aridity, and the Growth of the American West* (New York: Pantheon Books, 1985).

11. Alvin M. Josephy Jr., *Now That the Buffalo's Gone* (New York: Alfred A. Knopf, 1982); Francis Paul Prucha, *The Great Father: The United States Government and the American Indians* (Lincoln: University of Nebraska Press, 1985).

12. Rodolfo Acuna, *Occupied America: A History of Chicanos* (New York: Harper Collins, 1988); Albert Camarillo, *Chicanos in a Changing Society: From Mexican Pueblos to American Barrios in Santa Barbara and*

Southern California, 1848–1930 (Cambridge: Harvard University Press, 1979); Richard Griswold del Castillo, *The Treaty of Guadalupe Hidalgo: A Legacy of Conflict* (Norman: University of Oklahoma Press, 1990); Carey McWilliams, *North from Mexico: The Spanish Speaking People of the United States* (Philadelphia: J. B. Lippincott, 1948); Oscar Martinez, *Troublesome Border* (Tucson: University of Arizona Press, 1986).

13. Sucheng Chan, *Asian Americans: An Interpretive History* (Boston: Twayne, 1991); Ronald Takaki, *Strangers from a Different Shore: A History of Asian Americans* (Boston: Little, Brown, 1989).

14. Paul Wallace Gates, *History of Public Land Law Development* (Washington, D.C.: GPO, 1968); Roderick Nash, *Wilderness and the American Mind* (New Haven: Yale University Press, 1982); Charles F. Wilkinson, *Crossing the Next Meridian: Land, Water, and the Future of the West* (Washington, D.C.: Island Press, 1992).

15. Thomas Bender, "Wholes and Parts: The Need for Synthesis in American History," *Journal of American History* 73 (1986), 120–36.

16. White, "It's Your Misfortune and None of My Own," 58. White provides the most thorough discussion of the West and the rise of the federal government.

17. See ibid.

18. Earl Pomeroy, *In Search of the Golden West: The Tourist in Western America* (New York: Alfred A. Knopf, 1957); Henry Nash Smith, *Virgin Land: The American West as Symbol and Myth* (Cambridge: Harvard University Press, 1950); Richard Slotkin, *The Fatal Environment: The Myth of the Frontier in the Age of Industrialization, 1800–1890* (New York: Atheneum, 1985); idem, *Gunfighter Nation: The Myth of the Frontier in Twentieth-Century America* (New York: Atheneum, 1992); William H. Truettner, ed., *The West as America: Reinterpreting the Images of the Frontier, 1820–1920* (Washington, D.C.: Smithsonian Institution Press, 1991).

19. Tad Bartimus and Scott McCartney, *Trinity's Children: Living along America's Nuclear Highway* (New York: Harcourt Brace Jovanovich, 1991); Philip L. Fradkin, *Fallout: An American Nuclear Tragedy* (Tucson: University of Arizona Press, 1989); Carole Gallagher, *American Ground Zero: The Secret Nuclear War* (New York: Random House, 1991); Patricia Nelson Limerick, "The Significance of Hanford in American History," in *Washington Comes of Age*, ed. David Stratton (Pullman: Washington State University Press, 1994).

20. Charles Howard Shinn, *Mining Camps: A Study in American Fron-*

tier Government (1884; reprint, New York: Harper & Row, 1965), 3.

21. Limerick, "The Case of the Premature Departure."

22. Patricia Nelson Limerick, "The Adventures of the Frontier in the Twentieth Century," in *The Frontier in American Culture*, ed. James Grossman (Berkeley: University of California Press, 1994).

23. "Alive and Kickin'," written and sung by Roy Rogers, *Roy Rogers Tribute*, BMG Music 3024-4-R.

24. See, for instance, Mark Obmascik, "Alleged 'War on West' Resulting in More Wins Than Losses," *Denver Post*, 18 June 1994.

25. Carl Abbott, *The Metropolitan Frontier: Cities in the Modern American West* (Tucson: University of Arizona Press, 1993); John Findlay, *Magic Lands: Western Cityscapes and American Culture after 1940* (Berkeley: University of California Press, 1992).

Contributors

EDWARD L. AYERS is a specialist in Southern history. Born in western North Carolina and raised in eastern Tennessee, he received his graduate education in southern Connecticut and is now the Hugh P. Kelly Professor of History at the University of Virginia. His works include *Vengeance and Justice: Crime and Punishment in the Nineteenth-Century American South* (1984) and *The Promise of the New South: Life after Reconstruction* (1992).

PATRICIA NELSON LIMERICK is the author of *Desert Passages* (1985), *The Legacy of Conquest: The Unbroken Past of the American West* (1987), and, with Richard White, *The Frontier in American Culture* (1994). She is the coeditor of *Trails: Toward a New Western History* (1991) and *A Society to Match the Scenery* (1991). She received her Ph.D. from Yale University in 1980, taught at Harvard University from 1980 to 1984, and is now a professor of history at the University of Colorado, Boulder.

STEPHEN NISSENBAUM is a social and cultural historian and a professor of history at the University of Massachusetts, Amherst. His books include *Salem Possessed* (1974, with Paul Boyer), *Sex, Diet, and Debility in Jacksonian America* (1980), and *The Battle for Christmas* (forthcoming). He has held fellowships from the NEH, the ACLS, the American Antiquarian Society, and the Charles

Warren Center at Harvard University. Active in the public humanities, he has served as a member and president of the Massachusetts Foundation for the Humanities. He earned his Ph.D. at the University of Wisconsin.

PETER S. ONUF, Thomas Jefferson Memorial Foundation Professor of History at the University of Virginia, specializes in the political and constitutional history of the early American republic. Born in southern Connecticut and educated in Baltimore, Onuf taught at institutions in the West, New York, New England, and Texas before arriving in central Virginia. He is the author of *The Origins of the Federal Republic: Jurisdictional Controversies in the United States, 1775–1787* (1983) and *Federal Union, Modern World: The Law of Nations in the Age of Revolution, 1776–1814* (1993, with Nicholas G. Onuf).

Index

Library of Congress Cataloging-in-Publication Data
All over the map : rethinking American regions / Edward L. Ayers . . . [et al.].
    p.   cm.
  Includes index.
  ISBN 0-8018-5206-4 (hardbound : alk. paper)
  ISBN 0-8018-5392-3 (pbk. : alk. paper)
    1. Regionalism—United States—History.   2. Sectionalism (United States)—
History.   I. Ayers, Edward L., 1953–   .
  E179.5.A43   1996   95-21455
  306'.0973—dc20   CIP

Printed in the United States
39901LVS00002B/166-183